Metaphor as a Change Agent

Application of Metaphors
in Cognitive Restructuring

Ali Sahebi (Ph.D)

Serial Number: P2546160266
Title: Metaphor as a Change Agent
Sub Title: Application of Metaphors in Cognitive Restructuring
Author: Ali Sahebi (Ph.D)
Editor: Patricia kyle
Layout: Mehri Oskoei
Cover Design: Maryam Rashidzadeh
Redesign Illustration (Cover): Zohreh Sohani
ISBN: 978-1-77892-263-3
Subjects: Personal Transformation, Psychotherapy.
Format and Size: Paperback, 5.8 by 8.3 Inches
Pages: 288
Publication Date: November 2025
Publisher: Kidsocado International Publishing
Printed in the United States of America
Available in hardcover and ebook editions.

Copyright © 2025 Kidsocado International Publishing
All rights reserved, including the right of reproduction in whole or in part in any form.
Registered with the U.S. Copyright Office.

Kidsocado INTERNATIONAL PubLishiNG
VANCOUVER, CANAdA

Phone: +1 (236) 333-7248
WhatsApp: +1 (236) 333-7248
Email: info@kidsocado.com
Website: https://kidsocado.com
Address: 2100-1055 West Georgia St,
Vancouver, BC V6E 3P3, Canada

To Siavosh, Kiyanosh, and Sara

my beloved children, in whose curious eyes the light of stories forever flickers.

You have kept the lantern of storytelling aglow within me.

May tales guide your hearts, as they have long guided mine.

Acknowledgments

My heartfelt thanks go to my two kind, precise, and thoughtful sons. First, to Kiyanosh Sahebi, who typed the first draft of this book and offered encouraging feedback—all at the young age of 14. Second, to Siavosh Sahebi, now a thoughtful philosopher in his own right, who read the manuscript carefully before publication and provided insightful comments.

I am also deeply grateful to Harald Poynten, who read the entire text multiple times, offered critical feedback, and helped refine its structure and clarity through careful editing.

Finally, my sincere appreciation goes to Ms. Naghmeh Keshavarz, the devoted publisher of this book, whose open-mindedness and exceptional dedication brought it to life.

Thank you all—without your support, this work would not have been possible.

Contents

Introduction	9
What Is metaphor and What Is Its Application?	15
Abraham, the Fire, and the Sparrow	17
The Story of the Shepherd and the Counselor	21
The Parrot and the Grocer	26
How the Parrot Found His Way Out	30
The Crow and the Peacock	37
Standing on our Trainers' Shoulders	42
Defining Heaven and Hell	47
The Courage to Risk a Challenge	52
Expensive Thrift	56
The Long Trek	61
Shadows on the Sundial	66
Three Reaction Types	70
The Doctor Knows All	74
Not Everything at Once	78
The Perfect Camel	82
Big Rocks First	87
The Door	92
Gandhi's Completeness	96
The Food of Paradise	101
When the Waters Changed	105

Elephant in the Dark Room	109
How We Entrapped Ourselves?	112
Namouss the Shrewd	116
The Man Who Sold His House and Cat	121
Losing Yourself	124
How a Tradition Was Born	127
The Bird and the Egg	130
Logic Isn't Always Enough	133
"Two Paths, One Life"	137
The Water of Paradise	142
Jesus and the Doubters	146
The Parable of Greedy Sons	149
Hot Buttons	153
Jesus Escaping from Fools	156
The Fool and the Browsing Camel	161
Three Jeweled Rings	164
The Illusion of Devotion	168
Who Attain	172
Noticing Your Way to Freedom	175
The Literature Teacher in the Well	178
Nasruddin and the princess	182
The Dog's Vow in Winter, While Building Its House in Summer	185
Three Pieces of Advice	188
Still Carrying Her	192

The Fox and the Grapes	197
Overcoming Fear of Rejection	201
The Power of our View	206
Three Ways to Tolerance	210
The Wayward Princess	214
The Son Who Killed his Mother	219
The Toothless Cobra	223
Overcoming our Past Actions	226
Terrible Tempers	229
Don't Think of Monkeys	232
The Three Fish	235
Being on Top	239
Socrates and the Triple Filter Test	243
Love is Best	247
Two Wolves	253
The Most Important Part	256
The Ant and the Grasshopper: Minimizing Risk	260
The Pain of Pleasing Others	264
Unconditional Support as a Proactive Behavior	267
Nails in the Fence	271
Stress Management	275
The Daffodils	279
References	285
About Dr. Ali Sahebi	287

Introduction

Throughout human history, civilizations have utilized the power of stories and metaphors to share knowledge, wisdom, and insights between generations. The role of stories and metaphors in maintaining and advancing culture cannot be overstated. Metaphors and stories allow us to gain a deeper understanding of something by providing us with perspectives that we may not have access to in our ordinary lives. By taking on these metaphors, reflecting on them and grasping their meanings, we are able to internalize their lessons so as to foster meaningful change within ourselves. Metaphors are additionally powerful because they refuse to reveal their true meaning in a direct and obvious manner. Metaphors force us to look deeper than the mere words on the page. They demand that we truly think about the words and their underlying meanings before we can solve the puzzle placed before us.

The reason this is so powerful is that only once we take the time and put in the effort to think about something, to deeply reflect on its contents, can we come to a meaningful understanding of it. It is only once a meaningful understanding has been reached that we can begin to incorporate it into our own lives. Real behavioral change seldom comes from without. We must be willing to look within ourselves, to put in the hard labor of confronting our inner world, our thoughts, emotions and judgments. It is only when we reflect internally and explore what is within us that we can come to learn who we truly are, to gain true knowledge about ourselves. This knowledge about our true self is the first step in a long journey of self-directed behavioral change because we cannot change what we do not know. If we do not know why we think, feel or react in certain ways in particular situations then we have no way of understanding the underlying causes and therefore we are powerless to control or change them.

By exposing us to novel perspectives and ideas, stories and metaphors open the door for us to reflect on what we have read and to think about how they apply to us and our current situation. They can provide surprising insights which we may not have had access to or considered before and which can act as a catalyst for internal change. Additionally, in our current modern world full of distractions and often mindless stimuli we can often lose sight of what is important to us and some of the basic truths which helped our ancestors live meaningful and fulfilling lives. In this context, stories and metaphors can ground us in some of the simple yet profound truths of the human condition and provide us with a safe space where we can take the time to reflect for ourselves and for our own sake.

Metaphors and stories have always played a vital role in education. Encouraging students to explore different worlds in order to gain a deeper understanding of their outer and inner worlds has always been a key tenet of education. Stories allow us to learn from some of the greatest teachers history has to offer, and by taking on their perspectives and engaging in a deep, meaningful conversation with them, we can, incorporate their lessons into our own lives. By learning from their experiences, successes and mistakes, we can reflect on our own lives and learn more about ourselves, where we are in life, where we want to go and how we can achieve human flourishing for our own self.

From a psychological view, metaphors are the right brain's unique contribution to the left brain's language capability (Leonard shlain, 1988). Metaphors combine an inner logic and narrative sequence expressed through words (left brain preference) together with aspects of creativity, cohesion and **pattern forming** expressed through tone and emotion (right brain preference). In this way, both hemispheres of our brain are stimulated. From another perspective, metaphors are a form of social glue that serves to entertain, instruct, and challenge the listener or reader.

The use of stories and metaphors in therapy rooms provides a method to enhance information processing in sessions including vivid stories and metaphors, to help clients translate session material into behavioral change.

It is also reported that basic neuropsychology teaches us to use chunk information if we want to remember it. Moreover, research on the therapeutic use of imagery suggests that memory for verbal information is enhanced when the material is organized and interesting, is mildly but not severely emotionally evocative, and utilizes a number of sensory realms (Baddeley, 1990; Cahill, Prins, Weber, & McGaugh, 1994). Chunked information in a coherent, logical form that utilizes multiple senses and engages emotions: that sounds like a story to me.

Stories potentially allow an individual to externalize an issue and examine it more objectively. Likewise, stories may be used to provide a model of—a way to "think through"—the change process. One of the more popular stories in our program has been used as a primer for training in more adaptive cognitive skills.

Rather than relying exclusively on classic cognitive restructuring techniques which emphasize logical evaluation (e.g., Beck, 1995), we talk about coaching in the context of a story, for example, about Johnny, a Little League baseball player. This story has been formally incorporated into our treatment manual for using Panic Control Therapy strategies to aid benzodiazepine discontinuation (Otto, Jones, Craske, & Barlow, 1996).

This book contains a set of metaphors from a wide range of time periods and regions of the world. While the aim of this book and the choice of metaphors are to elicit deep reflection and contemplation, it must be admitted that work and labor is needed on your behalf, the reader, in order to extract the full value of this book. This is because merely reading these metaphors does not lead to greater learning and understanding on its own. What is needed is time and effort to sit back and think about what has been read, to understand what the words mean and what connection they are trying to make.

It is only then that the reader can begin to internalize the lessons of these metaphors and incorporate them into an effort toward meaningful behavioral change.

It is for the above reasons that I encourage the reader to take their time with this book, to give each story and metaphor enough time to leave its impression so that the reader may take what is most valuable for you and your life. The reality is that each reader may take a different lesson from each metaphor and different metaphors may have more or less impact and influence depending on the reader. This is totally expected as we are all different people, living different lives with different perspectives, and what each of us needs at any given time in our lives is different. Yet at the same time, readers will notice that there may be common lessons and takeaways from metaphors of different time periods and regions, and this is because despite our very real differences we also share the human experience in common and there are certain truths which endure regardless of who we are and where we are.

I hope that this book can bring to the fore of your mind some meaningful and deep insights which can assist you in your life and on your journey of self-knowledge, self-development and self-improvement. I hope that you take the time to reflect on these metaphors—whether in meditation, while cooking, during a walk or any other time or place where you can engage in contemplation—and that they bring value to your life. Socrates once said "the unexamined life is not worth living"—I hope that this book and the metaphors contained within help you to examine your worthwhile life.

What Is a Metaphor and What Is Its Application?

As literary scholars have stated, "metaphor" (allegory or parable) in its literal sense means to bring a likeness, to liken one thing to another, to depict or represent something, and to serve as a moral lesson or warning to others. When a speaker uses a wise story to express their message and substantiate a point, they are essentially employing allegory. For example, when Saadi says, "Training the unworthy is like rolling a pumpkin up a dome" or "A wise man is like an apothecary's drum—silent, yet filled with value—while a fool is like a warrior's drum—loud and hollow" (Gulistan, Chapter Eight: On Rules for Conversation), he is using allegorical expression.

An allegory is a narrative with two levels of meaning: the literal or surface meaning, which is the story itself, and the metaphorical or symbolic meaning, where characters, actions, or even themes correspond to deeper abstract concepts. Allegories often convey specific and distinct moral, philosophical, or political implications embedded within their symbolic framework. In such texts, the surface narrative is not the true message the narrator aims to convey; that intended meaning lies within a hidden, unspoken layer. Thus, the second layer may be regarded as the "real" story, and the true value of the allegory lies in uncovering this deeper layer. Interpreting this level requires insight and experience, as the surface story can conceal meaning as much as reveal it.

Allegory has extensive applications in psychology, psychiatry, and mental health sciences. By engaging attention and imagination, it provides a suitable platform for indirect learning and invites individuals to introspect and self-evaluate. Moreover, allegory has the unique capacity to make complex, layered, and abstract concepts simple, concrete, and universally accessible.

In Persian literature, Rumi's Masnavi Ma'navi stands out prominently in this regard. Many of its stories are allegorical or employ parables. These allegories carry both educational and artistic value. As A. J. Arberry noted, "Rumi is the master of allegorical storytelling in the world."

Abraham, the Fire, and the Sparrow

All eyes were anxiously fixed on Abraham and the blazing fire. Amid the chaos, a little sparrow was seen flying back and forth toward the flames.

Someone asked, "Little bird, what are you doing?"

The sparrow replied, "There is a spring nearby. I fill my beak with water and drop it over the fire."

They said, "But this fire is far too great for the few drops you carry. It won't make any difference."

The sparrow answered, "I may not be able to put out the fire but when God asks me: When My innocent servant was thrown into the fire, what did you do? I will say: I did all I could."

And blessed are the proud sparrows…

Motahhari, Morteza.

Suggested Reflection and Exercise
1. Personal Reflection:

Have you ever felt small or powerless in the face of a great injustice, crisis, or challenge? Reflect on a time when you tried to help—even in a small way—despite knowing your actions might not change the outcome. What motivated you? How did it make you feel?

2. Broader Perspective:

This story speaks to the importance of integrity, intention, and personal responsibility. Even when the odds are overwhelming, choosing action over indifference has spiritual and moral weight. It's not always about success but about standing for what is right. In a world full of "fires," the sparrow reminds us that every small act of courage counts.

3. Questions for Discussion or Writing:

- Why do you think the sparrow chose to act, even knowing it wouldn't extinguish the fire?

- What does this story teach us about personal responsibility and faith?

- How can small acts of good influence broader change in society?

- In what ways do we underestimate the value of "small" efforts?

- What is more important: the outcome of our actions or the intention behind them?

4. Suggested Practical Activity:

Now try to identify a current "fire" in your own community or world—a problem that seems too big to solve alone (e.g., climate change, bullying, injustice, war). Then, write or share one small action you can take this week, like the sparrow, to make a positive difference. Be brave enough to follow through and share your idea with people around you.

The Story of the Shepherd and the Counselor

A shepherd was busy grazing his flock of sheep in a remote meadow. Suddenly, the shiny new convertible car appeared through the dusty dirt roads. The driver of the car—a young man dressed in Brioni, Gucci shoes, Ray-Ban glasses, and a YSL tie—stuck his head out the window and asked, "If I tell you exactly how many sheep you have, will you give me one of them?"

The shepherd glanced at the newly wealthy young man and then at his peacefully grazing flock, and with a calm dignity, agreed.

The young man parked his car to the side, quickly took out his notebook computer, connected it to a remote phone line, accessed NASA's website where he could activate the satellite GPS system. He logically pinpointed the pasture, created a 60-page Excel workbook database, and entered complex formulas into the computer.

Finally, he printed 150 pages of output data from the system using a miniature printer he carried with him. Then, handing the papers to the shepherd, he said, "You have exactly 1,586 sheep here."

The shepherd replied, "That's correct. Now, as we agreed before, you can take one of the sheep."

Then he watched the young man as he carefully selected a sheep and placed it into his car. When the man finished selecting, the shepherd turned to him and said, "If I tell you exactly what your job is, will you give me back my sheep?"

The young man answered, "Yes, of course!"

The shepherd said, "You are a consultant."

The young man said, "You're right, but tell me how you guessed that!"

The shepherd replied, "It's simple. You came here without being asked, you charged me to answer a question I already knew the answer to, and moreover, you know nothing about my business—because instead of taking a sheep, you took the sheepdog."

Wilkinson, J. (2025).

Suggested Reflection and Exercise

1. Personal Reflection:

Have you ever been in a situation where someone offered elaborate advice or solutions that missed the real issue? Reflect on a time when simplicity and lived experience outperformed complexity and external expertise. How did it shape your view of practical wisdom versus theoretical knowledge?

2. Broader Perspective:

This story highlights the importance of humility, listening, and real-world understanding. It critiques modern tendencies to overanalyze or overengineer simple matters, often overlooking context, tradition, and practical expertise. In many fields, there's value in recognizing and respecting the insight of those who are directly engaged in the work.

3. Questions for Discussion or Writing:

- What does this story suggest about the difference between knowledge and wisdom?

- Why might highly educated people sometimes fail to understand real-life problems?

- How can we balance expertise with local or experiential knowledge in our workplaces or communities?

- Have you ever made a "consultant mistake"—solving the wrong problem?

- What qualities make someone a truly helpful advisor or problem-solver?

4. Suggested Practical Activity:

In pairs or small groups, share a time when an "expert" misunderstood a situation you knew well—or when you misunderstood someone else's situation because you lacked context. Then, brainstorm a short list of guidelines for being a thoughtful helper, such as: Ask before acting, listen deeply, clarify the real need, check assumptions. Post your list in your classroom or workspace.

The Parrot and the Grocer

A grocer had a beautiful green parrot in his shop. The parrot could speak like a human and converse with customers. It acted both as a guard for the store and as a charming entertainer who joked with people and made them laugh, helping attract customers.

One day, while the shopkeeper was away, the parrot tried to fly from one side of the shop to the other. In doing so, it accidentally knocked over a bottle of oil, spilling it everywhere and making a mess.

When the grocer returned and saw the oil all over the shop, he immediately realized it was the parrot's doing. In anger, he grabbed a stick and struck the parrot on the head. The blow injured the parrot, caused a wound, and made it lose all the feathers on its head, leaving it bald.

Since then, the parrot has not spoken .It said nothing at all. The grocer, full of regret, began to wish he hadn't hit the bird. He kept praying and making vows, hoping the parrot would recover and speak again so it could once more delight the customers with its talk.

After three days of silence, the grocer sat gloomily at the door of his shop. Just then, a bald man passed by—his shiny head resembling the surface of a copper bowl. Suddenly, the parrot broke its silence and said to the man:

"O bald man! What made you lose your hair and join the bald folk? Did you also spill a bottle of oil?"

The customers burst into laughter at the parrot's naive comparison. The parrot had assumed that anyone who was bald must have gone through the same experience—knocking over oil and getting punished.

One should not judge others based on personal experience alone. Even if similarities exist, it does not mean the causes or truths are the same. Just as the words for "lion" and "milk" in Persian may look similar in writing, their meanings are completely different.

(Rumi, Masnavi-e Manavi).

Suggested Reflection and Exercise

1. Personal Reflection:

Have you ever jumped to conclusions about someone else's situation based on your own experiences? How did that affect your relationship or your understanding of them?

2. Broader Perspective:

This story reminds us how our personal lens can distort reality. It teaches that while we may share outward similarities with others, the roots of our experiences can be entirely different. True understanding requires humility and curiosity, not projection.

3. Questions for Discussion or Writing:

- What are some examples in your life where misunderstanding others' circumstances led to conflict or embarrassment?

- Why do we tend to assume others' experiences mirror our own?

- How can we better train ourselves to ask rather than assume?

4. Suggested Practical Activity:

Choose one person you've made assumptions about recently. Without judgment, write down what you think you know about them—then list what you don't actually know. If appropriate, initiate a conversation to learn more about their story, practicing open, non-assumptive listening.

How the Parrot Found His Way Out

A merchant kept a beautiful, sweet-talking parrot in a cage. One day, as he prepared for a journey to India, he asked each of his servants and maids what souvenir they wanted him to bring back. Each of them requested something. The merchant then asked the parrot, "What shall I bring you from India?"

The parrot replied, "If you encounter parrots in India, tell them of my plight. Tell them I long to see them, but by ill fate, I am imprisoned in a cage. Convey my greetings and ask them for guidance. Ask them: 'Is it fitting that I yearn for you while dying of separation and loneliness in this cramped cage? Where is the loyalty of friends? Is it fair that I am in a cage while you are in gardens and meadows? O companions, remember this sorrowful, heartbroken bird. Remembering friends is sweet and beautiful for everyone. When you drink and eat, spill a drop on the earth in my memory.'"

The merchant promised to deliver the parrot's message to the Indian parrots.

When the merchant reached India, he saw several parrots on a tree in the wilderness. He halted his horse, greeted them, and relayed his parrot's message. Upon hearing it, one of the parrots suddenly trembled, fell from the tree, and died instantly. The merchant regretted delivering the message and thought, "I caused this poor parrot's death! Surely this parrot was related to mine, or they shared one soul in two bodies. Why did I speak and kill this innocent? Our words are like stone and iron—we must not strike them together needlessly. The world is dark like a cotton field; why set it aflame? Tyrants are those who close their eyes and set the world on fire with their words. Words are so powerful that with a single one, you can burn a whole world or rouse a dead fox to roar like a lion."

The merchant successfully concluded his business and returned home. He brought gifts for everyone in the household. After distributing them, the parrot asked, "What about my souvenir? Did you deliver my message? What did the parrots say? Tell me what you told them and what you heard."

The merchant said, "Truthfully, I deeply regret delivering that message and decided not to speak of it. I still wrestle with why I, the fool, did such a thing. Never again will I speak carelessly."

The parrot insisted, "Why do you regret it? What happened? Why are you upset?"

The merchant remained silent, but the parrot persisted until he relented, "When I told your message to the parrots, one of them, overcome by grief for you, trembled upon hearing your plight, fell from the tree, and died. I truly regret speaking your words—but regret is useless. A word once spoken is like an arrow released from a bow; it cannot be taken back."

As soon as the parrot heard this, it trembled, fell to the bottom of the cage, and died. The merchant screamed in anguish, threw his hat to the ground, tore his clothes, and cried, "O my sweet-voiced bird! Why did this happen? Woe is me—my eloquent bird is dead! O tongue, you have brought me nothing but loss!"

The merchant wailed bitterly for the parrot. After much lamentation and remorse, he opened the cage, took the parrot out, and laid it on the floor. Suddenly, the parrot flew up and perched on a nearby tree branch.

Astonished, the merchant asked, "O beautiful bird, explain yourself to me! What did that Indian parrot do that you learned to deceive me?"

The parrot said, "By its action, it advised me to abandon speaking, singing, and dancing. They caged you for your sweet voice; to be free, you must change this trait. Play dead like I did, and they will release you. If you are a seed, birds will eat you; if you are a bud, children will pluck you. Whoever displays their beauty and talent invites a hundred calamities. Friends and foes alike will cast evil eyes upon them; envious schemers will plot against them."

From the tree, the parrot gave the merchant several pieces of advice, then bid him farewell and left.

The merchant called out, "Go! May God protect you. You showed me the path of truth—I shall follow it. My soul is no less than a parrot's. To liberate one's soul, one must abandon everything."

(Rumi: Masnavi-e Manavi).

Suggested Reflection and Exercise
1. Personal Reflection:
This story invites you to reflect on the cost of visibility, the power of silence, and the price of freedom.

- Have you ever felt trapped—physically, emotionally, or socially—like the caged parrot?

- Have your gifts or your voice ever led to unwanted attention or even limitations?

- What have you learned from observing others, without them saying a word?

2. Broader Perspective:

This allegory explores themes of expression vs. suppression, captivity vs. freedom, and wisdom gained through indirect communication. It challenges the idea that liberation always comes through action or protest—sometimes it comes through restraint, patience, or imitation. The story also questions whether society truly values authenticity, or punishes it.

3. Questions for Discussion or Writing:

- What does the parrot's transformation—from a caged singer to a silent escapee—teach us about adapting to one's environment?

- How does this story challenge the value of speech and performance in our lives?

- Was the Indian parrot's act truly compassionate or was it self-preserving?

- What role does suffering play in awakening wisdom or change in the story?

- What does the ending reveal about the relationship between freedom and ego?

4. Suggested Practical Activity:

"Silent Wisdom" Exercise

- Choose one full hour in your day to remain completely silent—no talking, no texting, no writing.

- During this hour, notice how others respond. Observe your environment without reacting.

- Reflect afterward: What did you learn about yourself, your habits, and your "cage"?

- Optional: Write a letter to your "inner parrot"—the part of you that longs for freedom but doesn't know how to escape.

The Crow and the Peacock

In the garden of a palace, a black crow perched upon the branch of an orange tree. He watched as, down on the manicured lawn below, a peacock strutted proudly back and forth.

The crow exclaimed, "Who allowed such a strange creature to enter this garden? He who walks around so pompous and lordly as if he were the king himself; a king with feet of wrinkled leather! And feathers such a garish shade of blue! What bird of sound mind would present himself in such a way? Yet here he stands, dragging his tail around behind him like a devious fox."

The crow stopped, eyes full of contempt. He waited for the peacock for reply. The peacock stood silent for a long moment.

He began dejectedly, "I'm not convinced by your protestations, crow. Mocking me only betrays your own ignorance. You call me arrogant because I hold my head high so that my feathers stand tall. But do not mistake the way I carry myself with pride. I know of my blemishes; I know of the wrinkles and discolorations on my feet that mar me. It pains me so much that I hold my head high—high enough so that I might not see my own feet. From your perch you see only what is most unpleasant to you. So your eyes are blind to my splendor. Has this escaped your notice, crow? If only you could see that what you ridicule as ugly is precisely what people admire in me."

This exchange reveals a profound truth about human perception: judgments often arise not from what others show, but from what we are unwilling or unable to see within ourselves. The crow's contempt reflects his blindness to his own insecurities, while the peacock's grace comes from acknowledging imperfection yet embracing one's unique strengths.

Idries Shah (1967).

Suggested Reflection and Exercise

1. Personal Reflection:

Think about a time when you judged someone quickly based on their appearance or behavior. How did that judgment affect your relationship or feelings toward them?

2. Broader Perspective:

Consider how your judgments might reflect your own fears or insecurities. What might you be avoiding seeing or accepting about yourself?

3. Questions for Discussion or Writing:

- How does acknowledging our own imperfections change the way we view others?

- Can pride sometimes be a protective mechanism? How?

- In what ways can embracing vulnerability lead to greater self-acceptance and compassion?

Suggested Practical Activity:

- Active Empathy Practice:

In the coming week, when you encounter a behavior or comment that upsets or frustrates you, pause for a moment before reacting. Ask yourself:

- What might this person be feeling or struggling with beneath the surface?

- Could my reaction be influenced by my own fears or biases?

- How can I respond with understanding rather than judgment?

Standing on our Trainers' Shoulders

A crowd of excited townspeople were packed into a traveling puppeteer's tent, watching his performance intently. At the very back of the congregation stood a father with his son. While the father, when on the tips of his toes, could just barely make out the scenes, his son's head barely reached the waists of those around him. The boy stretched and jumped to no avail. Finally, he cried until his father put him on his shoulders. He was delighted! Raised high above all others, the child could now watch the puppet show unimpeded, and was content.

He shouted with joy and jumped up and down on his father's shoulders, as if he was a rider and his father the horse. He pounded his fists on his father's head and kicked his feet against his chest; indeed, for a moment, he completely forgot that he was sitting on his father.

He stilled at the sight of a hand on his shoulder. He was scared and turned around to see an old man, grey and bearded, smiling softly at him.

"My son," said the man, "I see you are enjoying yourself very much. Your view of the show is better than any anyone else in this tent. But consider this: if your father hadn't taken the trouble to put you on his shoulders, you would still be standing down below, unable to see. So don't forget whose shoulders you are resting on. You should enjoy and be happy. But you should also think of the person upon whose shoulders you happily sit."

Owen (2000).

Suggested Reflection and Exercise
1. Personal Reflection:
- Think of someone in your life—perhaps a mentor, teacher, parent, or elder—who has supported or lifted you in some way. How did their help change your perspective or open up opportunities for you?

- Have you ever taken someone's support for granted, even unintentionally?

2. Broader Perspective:
- Societies, knowledge, and cultures grow by building on what came before. In what ways do you benefit today from the efforts or sacrifices of past generations?

- How might this awareness shape the way you lead, teach, or support others?

3. Questions for Discussion or Writing:
- What does it mean to "sit on someone's shoulders"?

- How can we honor or give back to those who have elevated us?

- How can we remain humble and grateful even when we're in positions of advantage?

4. Suggested Practical Activity:

- **Gratitude Letter:** Write a short letter (or message) to someone who helped raise you up—literally or metaphorically. Tell them how their support impacted your life. If they're no longer living, write the letter anyway and reflect on how you might carry their legacy forward.

- **Mentorship Awareness:** In the coming week, look for ways you can offer support or encouragement to someone younger or less experienced—just as others once did for you.

Defining Heaven and Hell

An orthodox believer desired to know the nature of heaven and hell, so that he might live his life according to what resides in each. He approached the prophet, Elijah.

"Where is hell and where is heaven?" Asked the believer.

Elijah did not answer him.

Instead of telling him, Elijah took the man by the hand and led him through the gates of a huge, many-spired palace. They passed through a towering iron door and entered a large room filled with many people of every walk and facet of life. Great lords and noblemen stood adorned in jewels and embroidered robes, beside men in rags. At the room's center a pot of soup rested over an open fire. A welcoming smell emanated from the boiling casserole within and spread throughout the room. Around the pot, crowds of desperate people with sunken cheeks and hollow eyes, moved to get their share of soup.

The man who had come along with Elijah was amazed when he saw the spoons that people carried: they were as tall as the people themselves. Each spoon consisted of an iron bowl, burning hot from the heat of the soup, and at the very end a small wooden handle. The hungry people huddled around the pot impatiently. Although each wanted his or her share, no one got it.

It was hard to lift the heavy spoon out of the pot, and since the spoon was very big and the handle only tiny, even the strongest men could not raise their spoons to their mouths. In their self-absorbed desperation, many burned their arms and faces, or spilled the soup on their neighbors. In anger, they fought and hit each other with the spoons they should have been using to relieve their hunger.

The prophet Elijah drew his companion close and warned, "This is hell!"

They left the room, and soon the infernal cries and shouting behind them died. After a long journey through dark passages, they entered a different room. Here too, many people of many walks of life sat around. In the middle of the room there was again a pot of hot soup. Each person there had a gigantic spoon in his hand, just like the ones Elijah and the man had seen in hell. But here the people seemed well nourished and content. Only a quiet, satisfied humming could be heard, along with the sounds of the spoons being dipped into the soup. The man noticed that there were always two people working together. One would dip the spoon into the pot and feed his partner. If the spoon became too heavy for one person, others would come to their aid, so that everyone was able to eat in peace. As soon as one person had enough to eat, it was another's turn.

The prophet Elijah turned to his companion, "This is heaven."

Idries Shah (1967).

Suggested Reflection and Exercise

1. Personal Reflection:

- Reflect on moments when you focused solely on your own needs or desires without considering others. How did that affect your relationships or well-being?

- Think about times when cooperation or helping others brought you a deeper sense of satisfaction or peace. What made those experiences different?

2. Broader Perspective:

- How does this story redefine the traditional ideas of "heaven" and "hell"?

- What does it say about the nature of suffering and joy in community life?

- How might our personal or social "heavens" and "hells" be shaped by how we treat and support each other?

3. Questions for Discussion or Writing:
- Why do you think people in "hell" in the story hurt themselves and each other despite being so close to nourishment?

- What practical steps can we take to build "heaven" in our families, workplaces, or communities?

- How can awareness of interdependence change the way we approach daily challenges?

4. Suggested Practical Activity:

- **Mutual Support Mapping:** Identify three people in your life with whom you can practice mutual support—whether emotional, practical, or otherwise. Make a plan to check in regularly and help one another, just like the people sharing the soup.

- **Empathy Reflection:** When you face frustration or scarcity this week, pause and ask yourself: Am I holding on too tightly? How can sharing or cooperating ease this situation?

The Courage to Risk a Challenge

A king called together the men of his court for a test of their abilities. He who could solve it was promised great rewards. In no time at all, powerful and wise men surrounded him in great numbers.

"You wise men," spoke the king, "I have a problem, and I wish to see which of you is able to solve it."

He led the men to an enormous door, bigger than anyone had ever seen.

The king explained, "Here you see the largest and heaviest door in my kingdom. Who amongst you can open it?"

Some of the powerful men just shook their heads. Some of the wise men inspected the door more closely, but admitted they couldn't do it. When the wise men had said this, the rest of the court concurred that this was too difficult a problem for them to solve. Then, a single figure approached the door. This man studied the door and ran his hands across it to try and find any weakness; finally, he pulled on it with a powerful tug and the door opened.

It had been left ajar, and nothing more had been needed but the willingness to realize that and the courage to act boldly. The king spoke, "You will get the position I offered. You alone do not rely just on what you see or hear; you put your own powers into action and are willing to risk a challenge."

Owen (2000).

Suggested Reflection and Exercise
1. Personal Reflection:
- Recall a time when you faced a problem that seemed too big or difficult. Did you hesitate or try to find an easier way around it? What stopped you from trying?

- Reflect on moments when a simple action or a shift in perspective helped you overcome a challenge. How did courage and willingness play a role?

2. Broader Perspective:
- How does this story challenge common assumptions about difficulty and effort?

- What does it say about the importance of action versus overthinking or relying solely on others' opinions?

- In what ways can fear of failure or the unknown keep us from discovering simple solutions?

3. Questions for Discussion or Writing:

- Why do you think many wise and powerful men failed to open the door while the single man succeeded?

- How can courage to act be cultivated in daily life or in professional settings?

- What "doors" in your life might be "ajar" but waiting for you to notice and push?

4. Suggested Practical Activity:

- **Door-Opening Challenge:** Identify one task or problem you have been avoiding because it feels too difficult. This week, take a small but bold step towards it—no need to solve it fully, just move forward with courage and curiosity.

- **Perspective Shift:** Practice looking at a challenge from a fresh angle—ask yourself: What if the solution is simpler than I imagine? What if I just try, even if it feels risky?

Expensive Thrift

A man charged with theft stood before the court. All indications were that he was guilty. The judge that stood before him was known to be a rational and compassionate man. He gave the offender a choice of three punishments: the offender could pay a fine of 2000 dollars, suffer fifty blows with a stick, or eat five kilograms of onions. The onions did not sound so terrible, thought the convicted man, and thus he chose the latter punishment.

After having eaten the first four kilograms of raw onions, he shivered with disgust at the sight of them growing in the field. His eyes were overflowing, a flood of tears poured down his cheeks.

"Your Honour," the man pleaded, "I beg you to bring this to an end – I would rather receive the stick blows." The man thought he would be able to save his money by being cunning, he was notorious amongst his friends for his stinginess.

The court servant removed the thief's clothes and stretched him out over the bench. Just the sight of the muscular court servant and the flexible rod made the man tremble. With every blow to his back he screamed louder, until at the tenth blow he finally moaned, "Glorious Judge, have pity on me; stop the blows." The judge nodded his head.

At that, the offender, who had wanted to spare himself the blows and save his money, and who had finally tasted all three punishments, begged, "Let me instead pay the two thousand dollars."

Peseschkian (1987).

Suggested Reflection and Exercise
1. Personal Reflection:

- Think about times when trying to avoid discomfort or cost led you to face even bigger challenges. How did hesitation or false economy affect your choices?

- Reflect on moments when facing a problem directly—though difficult—saved you from longer-term consequences.

2. Broader Perspective:

- What does this story reveal about the value of choosing wisely and accepting discomfort early?

- How can avoidance or trying to "game the system" sometimes lead to greater hardship?

- In what ways do we sometimes underestimate the true cost of our decisions?

3. Questions for Discussion or Writing:

- Why did the man choose to eat the onions first? What does that choice say about human nature and risk assessment?

- How does fear of immediate pain or loss affect decision-making in everyday life?

- Can you think of examples where short-term "savings" turned into long-term expenses, either financially, emotionally, or socially?

4. Suggested Practical Activity:

- **Facing the Onion Challenge:** Identify a small discomfort or difficult task you've been avoiding, perhaps to save time, money, or energy. This week, commit to confronting it early, and observe how that affects your stress or outcomes.

- **Cost Reflection:** Keep a journal for a few days and note moments when you try to avoid a problem. Reflect on whether avoidance helps or worsens the situation, and what alternative actions you could take.

The Long Trek

Persian mysticism tells of a wayfarer who wandered tirelessly along a road that stretched on for many miles, seeming never to end. The many objects that he had brought for the journey encumbered him terribly. A sack of sand hung on his back and a water hose dangled around his body. In his right hand, he carried an oddly shaped stone, in the left hand a boulder. Around his neck an old millstone dangled on a frayed rope. Rusty chains, with which he dragged leaden weights through the dusty sand, had wounded his ankles. On his head, the man was balancing a half-rotten pumpkin. With every step he took, the chains rattled. Moaning and groaning, he moved forward at a leaden pace, one step at a time. He constantly complained of his predicament and the exhaustion that tormented him.

On his way, a farmer met him in the glowing heat of the midday sun.

The bemused farmer asked, "Oh, tired wanderer, why do you weigh yourself down with that boulder?"

"Awfully foolish of me," remarked the wanderer, "but I hadn't noticed it before."

With that, he tossed aside the rock and immediately felt much lighter.

Again, after he had gone a long way further down the road, he encountered another farmer.

"Tell me, tired wanderer, why do you trouble yourself with the half-rotten pumpkin on your head, and why do you drag those heavy iron weights behind you on chains?"

The wanderer answered, "I'm very glad you pointed that out to me. I did not realize what I was doing to myself!"

He released himself from the chains and smashed the pumpkin into the ditch alongside the road. Once more his burden was lessened. But the further he went, the more he began to suffer again.

A farmer coming from his field watched him in amazement and called out, "Oh, good man, you are carrying sand in the sack, but what you see far off in the distance is more sand than you could ever carry. And your big water hose – this is as if you planned to cross the Kavir Desert. All this time there's a clear stream flowing alongside you, which will accompany you for much of your journey."

Upon hearing this, the wanderer tore open the water hose and emptied its brackish water onto the path. Then he filled a hole with the sand from his knapsack. He stood there pensively and looked into the sinking sun. The last rays illuminated him. He glanced down at himself, saw the heavy millstone around his neck, and suddenly realized it was the stone that was causing him to bend over and walk. He unloosed it and threw it as far as he could into the river. Freed from his burdens, he wandered on through the cool of the evening to find a home.

Idries Shah (1971).

Suggested Reflection and Exercise
1. Personal Reflection:
- Think about the "burdens" or limiting beliefs you carry in your own life. What are some "boulders" or "chains" you might be holding on to without realizing?

- Recall a time when letting go of something heavy—whether a habit, thought, or relationship—brought you relief or new freedom.

2. Broader Perspective:
- How does this story illustrate the importance of awareness in reducing self-imposed suffering?

- What does it say about how we often carry unnecessary burdens simply because we are unaware or habituated?

- How can mindfulness or self-reflection help us identify and release these burdens?

3. Questions for Discussion or Writing:

- Why do you think the wanderer did not notice his burdens at first?

- What roles do others (like the farmers) play in helping us see what we cannot see ourselves?

- How might this story relate to emotional or psychological "weights" people carry?

4. Suggested Practical Activity:
- **Burden Inventory:** Take a moment to write down any thoughts, worries, grudges, or habits that feel heavy or draining. For each, ask yourself, "Is this burden mine to carry? Is it necessary or can I set it down?"

- **Mindful Letting Go:** Choose one burden you feel ready to release. Imagine yourself putting it down or throwing it away like the wanderer did. Reflect on how this changes your mood or mindset.

Shadows on the Sundial

A king once wanted to impress his subjects in the East. Since they did not know what a clock was, he decided to bring back a sundial from his travels.

His gift altered the lives of the people in his kingdom. They began to understand the different parts of the day and to divide up their time accordingly. Becoming more orderly, reliable, and hardworking, they produced great wealth that allowed every man and woman to live more lavishly. When the king died, his subjects wondered how they could pay tribute to his achievements. Because the sundial symbolized the king's generosity and was the cause of much success, they decided to build around it a splendid temple with a golden dome. But when the temple was finished and the dome rose above the sundial, the rays of the sun no longer reached the dial. The sundial faded and the once-punctual subjects now had no way to tell the time. None of the citizens were reliable or hardworking any longer. Each of them went their own separate way. Within weeks, the kingdom collapsed into anarchy.

Peseschkian (1987).

Suggested Reflection and Exercise

1. Personal Reflection:

- Reflect on any tools, habits, or values in your life that help you stay focused and organized. Have you ever allowed distractions or obstacles to block their effectiveness?

- Consider times when success or external rewards made you lose sight of the original purpose or meaning behind your efforts.

2. Broader Perspective:

- How does this story illustrate the danger of obstructing the very foundations of success?

- What does it say about the balance between honoring achievements and maintaining their practical function?

- How might this apply to organizations, communities, or societies today?

3. Questions for Discussion or Writing:

- Why do you think the people built the temple around the sundial instead of preserving its function?

- How can symbols or traditions sometimes unintentionally hinder progress or clarity?

- What lessons can leaders learn from this story about celebrating success without losing sight of core values?

4. Suggested Practical Activity:

- **Assess Your Foundations:** Identify one key habit, tool, or value that supports your daily success or well-being. Reflect on any ways it might be "blocked" or undermined by other commitments or distractions.

- **Clear the Way:** Make a concrete plan to "clear the sun" on this foundation—whether by adjusting priorities, setting boundaries, or simplifying your environment—to help it shine fully again.

Three Reaction Types

A father plagued by concerns complained to his doctor, "My youngest son has made me old before my time. Worries fill my head. Yet my eldest son is the pillar of my life. Every word that leaves his mouth is a word of truth. He has never spoken a lie. The truth is as distant from my second son as the sun and stars above us. Every word he says is a lie. I've come to terms with it, because I always know what to expect from him. But my youngest son! He has no firm ground under his feet. He lies, and then a moment later he tells the truth. Every word from his mouth may be a lie or the truth, and I can't tell the difference. With the others, I know where I stand. This knowledge escapes me with my youngest son."

Mehdevi, A. S. (1980).

Suggested Reflection and Exercise

1. Personal Reflection:

- Think about people in your life whose behavior feels predictable versus those who are more unpredictable. How does this affect your trust and peace of mind?

- Reflect on moments when uncertainty in relationships has caused you stress or growth.

2. Broader Perspective:

- What does this story reveal about human nature and our need for consistency?

- How do certainty and unpredictability affect our emotional well-being and relationships?

- Can ambiguity sometimes lead to new insights or deeper understanding?

3. Questions for Discussion or Writing:
- Why might the father find the youngest son's unpredictable truthfulness more distressing than constant lying?

- How do we cope with uncertainty in relationships or life situations?

- What are the benefits and challenges of embracing ambiguity?

4. Suggested Practical Activity:
- **Embrace Uncertainty Exercise:** Over the next week, notice moments when you feel discomfort due to unpredictability—whether in people, events, or your own thoughts. Instead of resisting, take a few deep breaths and ask, "What might I learn from this uncertainty?"

- **Journal Your Insights:** Write down any new perspectives or feelings that arise from facing unpredictability without immediate judgment.

The Doctor Knows All

A man lay in bed, struck by a mysterious and debilitating illness, it appeared that his death was near. In her fear, his wife summoned the town doctor. For more than half an hour the doctor tapped around on the patient and listened; he checked his pulse, put his head to the man's chest, turned him onto his stomach and then his side and back again, raised the man's legs and torso, opened his eyes, looked into his mouth.

He then said with a heavy sadness, "Ma'am, unfortunately I must give you the grave news that your husband has been dead for 2 days."

At this very moment the ailing man raised his head in shock and whimpered, "No, my dearest, I'm still alive."

The wife gave her husband a powerful slap on the head and angrily remarked, "Be quiet, the doctor is an expert, he ought to know."

Peseschkian (1987).

Suggested Reflection and Exercise
1. Personal Reflection:
- Recall a time when you or someone you know doubted expert opinions and turned out to be right or wrong. How did that affect your trust?

- Reflect on your own relationship with authority and expertise. When do you feel comfortable questioning it?

2. Broader Perspective:
- What does this story suggest about the limits of expertise and the danger of blind trust?

- How do we balance respect for knowledge with our own intuition and observations?

- How might relying solely on authority affect decision-making?

3. Questions for Discussion or Writing:
- Why do you think the wife trusted the doctor over her husband's own voice?

- How can we cultivate healthy skepticism without falling into cynicism?

- What role does personal experience play alongside professional knowledge?

4. Suggested Practical Activity:

- **Questioning Authority Practice:** When you next receive advice or information from an expert or authority figure, pause and ask yourself, "Does this align with what I observe or feel? What else might I consider before accepting this?"

- **Journal Your Reflections:** Note any moments where you balanced respect for expertise with your own judgment and what outcomes followed.

Not Everything at Once

A priest entered a hall with the intention of giving a sermon. He found the hall to be empty with the exception of a young groom who sat in the very front row.

The priest, considering whether to proceed with his sermon or not, decided to ask the groom, "You are the only one here. Do you think I should speak or not?"

The groom responded to him, "I am a simple man and do not understand these things. But if I came into the stables and saw that all the horses had run off and only one remained, I would feed it anyway."

The priest was warmed by the sentiment and began to preach. His sermon went for over two hours. Afterwards, feeling satisfied, he wanted his audience's confirmation of how passionate and stirring his speech had been.

He asked, "How did you like my sermon?"

The groom answered, "I told you already that I am a simple man and do not understand these things very well. Yet if I came into the stables and found all the horses gone except one, I would feed it, but I wouldn't give it all the grain I had."

Moment of Christ—https://moments4christ.wordpress.com.

Suggested Reflection and Exercise

1. Personal Reflection:

- Think about a time when you wanted to give your full attention or effort but felt it was more than someone could handle at once. How did you adjust?

- How do you approach patience and pacing in your own life—do you tend to rush or take things step by step?

2. Broader Perspective:

- What does this story suggest about the importance of timing and moderation when sharing knowledge or help?

- How might overwhelming others, even with good intentions, be counterproductive?

- In what ways can patience improve communication and relationships?

3. Questions for Discussion or Writing:

- Why do you think the groom chose to stay and listen despite being alone and perhaps unfamiliar with sermons?

- How can we recognize when someone is ready to receive more or less from us?

- What are some ways to balance enthusiasm with sensitivity to others' capacity?

4. Suggested Practical Activity:
- **Pacing Practice:** In your next conversation or teaching moment, observe the other person's reactions and adjust the amount of information or intensity accordingly.

- **Reflection Journal:** Write about a situation where pacing your input made a difference in how your message was received.

The Perfect Camel

Many years ago, four scholars traveled through the Kavir desert with a caravan. In the evening they sat together beside the fire and told tales from their colorful lives. They all had great respect for the camels that helped them traverse the desert. They were amazed at the contentedness of the creatures. They admired their strength, and they agreed that their modesty and patience were unrivaled amongst men and animals.

"We are all masters of the written word." one declared.

"Let us use our talents to tell of the achievements of the camel and so give them the praise and honor that they deserve."

Saying these words, he took up a roll of parchment and retired to his tent, lighting an oil lamp so that he might work late into the night. After he had completed his work, he came out and presented it to his three friends. He had drawn a camel just getting up from a resting position. The camel was so detailed and life-like that one would almost think it was alive.

The next man then went into the tent and soon came out. He brought with him a short factual description of all the advantages that camels bring to a caravan. The third wrote an eloquent and delightful poem. Then the fourth man finally went into the tent and asked that the others should not to disturb him. A few hours later, the fire had died out, and the other scholars were asleep. But from the dimly lit tent, there still came the incessant scratching of the pen and the humming of a simple song.

The next day, the three waited excitedly for their companion, and again on the following two days when he didn't show himself, their intrigue only grew stronger. The tent shrouded the fourth scholar and his enigmatic work in secrecy and the others dared not interrupt his mysterious scribbling. Finally, on the fifth day, the entrance to the tent opened up, and the fourth scholar trudged out, eyes ringed with black circles and hair disheveled. A stubbly beard framed his chin. With exhausted steps and a pained look on his face, he approached the other men. He wearily threw a bundle of parchments onto the carpet. On the outside of the first roll he had written in large letters, as if denoting the title, "The perfect camel, or how a camel should be…."

Peseschkian (2016).

Suggested Reflection and Exercise

1. Personal Reflection:

- Have you ever worked hard on something that others completed quickly but differently? How did that make you feel?

- When you create or accomplish something, do you focus more on detail, function, or beauty? Why?

2. Broader Perspective:

- What does the story say about different approaches to honoring or understanding something?

- How do different perspectives enrich a shared goal or project?

- Can effort and dedication sometimes lead to burnout? How might balance be important?

3. Questions for Discussion or Writing:

- Why do you think the fourth scholar took so much longer than the others?

- What might the title "The perfect camel, or how a camel should be…" suggest about his work or mindset?

- How do you value precision and idealism versus practicality and efficiency?

4. Suggested Practical Activity:

- **Explore Perspectives:** Choose a common object or idea and try to describe it in three different ways: visually, factually, and poetically.

- **Balance Reflection:** Reflect on a task where you spent a lot of time perfecting details—was it worth it? What would you do differently next time?

Big Rocks First

A professor renowned across all of China welcomed a new class of students into a small room of their prestigious university. In front of him was a large glass jar, clear with a light green tinge to it. The same type of lights that some people might use to keep plants.

The professor looked at the students but said nothing. Then he leaned down to his right-hand side. By his foot was a pile of fist-sized rocks. He took a rock and very carefully dropped it through the hole at the top of the neck of the jar. They dropped one after another, until no more rocks could be dropped through the hole at the top of the jar.

He turned to the group and asked, "Tell me, is the jar now full?"

The group murmured and agreed: the jar was now full.

The professor said nothing and turned to his left side. By his foot was a pile of pebbles. He took a handful of pebbles and carefully poured them through the hole at the top of the neck of the jar, handful by handful, until no more pebbles could be poured through the hole at the top of the jar.

He turned to the group and said once more, "Tell me, is the jar now full?"

The group mumbled that it certainly appeared as if the jar could possibly now be full.

The professor said nothing and turned again to his right side. By his foot was a pile of dry sand. He took a handful of sand and carefully poured it through the hole at the top of the jar. He poured around the rocks and around the pebbles, until no more sand could be poured through the hole at the top of the jar.

He turned to the group and said: "Tell me, is the jar now full?"

No answer.

The professor said nothing and turned again to his left side. By his foot was a jug of water. He took the jug and carefully poured the water through the hole at the top of the jar, around the rocks, the pebbles, and the sand. He stopped once no more water could be poured through the hole at the top of the jar.

"Tell me, is the jar now full?"

There was total silence, even more profound than before. The kind of silence where those who are present check to see if their nails are clean or their shoes are polished. The professor turned again to his right side. On a small blue square of paper he had a small pile of fine, dry salt. He took a pinch of salt and carefully dissolved it in the water at the top of the jar. He sprinkled it in the water, around the sand, around the pebbles, around the rocks, until no more salt could be dissolved in the water at the top of the jar.

"Tell me, is the jar now full?"

Before they could respond, he exclaimed, "It is now most certainly full!"

The professor then invited all the people who were there to consider the meaning of his story. What was the meaning of all this? How did they interpret it? Why had the professor shown them this? And after some minutes, the professor listened to their reflections. There were as many interpretations as there were people in the room.

When the professor had heard from each of the students, he congratulated them, saying that it was hardly surprising there were so many different interpretations. After all, everybody there was a unique individual who had lived through unique experiences unlike those of anybody else. Their interpretations simply reflected their own lived experience and the particular and unique perspective through which they understood the world. In that sense, he assured them, no interpretation was any better, or any worse, than any other. He then asked whether the group was curious to know his own interpretation, which of course, he stated, was no better or worse than theirs. It was simply his interpretation.

Oh yes, they were curious.

"Well," he said, "my interpretation is simply this. Whatever you do in life, whatever the context, just make sure you get your rocks in first."

Covey (2025).

Suggested Reflection and Exercise

1. Personal Reflection:

Think about the "rocks" in your life—those big priorities or values that must come first. What are they for you? Are you sometimes so caught up in smaller tasks (the "pebbles" and "sand") that you forget to focus on what truly matters? How do you balance these different layers of your life?

2. Broader Perspective:

Consider how this story applies to time management, relationships, or personal goals in society. How might focusing on what's truly important help communities or organizations thrive? What happens when people prioritize less important things first?

3. Questions for Discussion or Writing:

- What do the rocks, pebbles, sand, water, and salt symbolize in your life?

- How can we make sure we "get our rocks in first" in a busy world?

- Can you think of a time when you ignored the "rocks" and later regretted it?

Suggested Practical Activity:
- **Priority Mapping:** Make a list of your current priorities. Identify your "rocks" (the most important), "pebbles" (medium importance), and "sand" (less important). Reflect on whether you are giving enough time to your rocks, and make a plan to adjust your focus this week.

The Door

A captain of industry was looking for a bright manager who would have the skills and insight to take over the running of his organization after his retirement. He assembled the best managers from his own company and hired numerous recruitment consultants and head-hunters to find him additional ones who might serve his purpose.

On a particular day, all the possible contenders were assembled in a great hall of an old building downtown which the organization had hired for that day. The captain of industry addressed the handpicked managers assembled before him.

"I have a problem, and I want to know who among you has the ability to solve it. What you see in the wall behind me is the biggest, mightiest and heaviest door you will ever see. Who amongst you, without assistance, has the power to open it?"

Some of the managers simply shook their heads. It was just too daunting a problem. Others examined the door more closely, discussed aspects of force and mass, remembered theories of problem solving they had learned in business school, and admitted that it seemed an impossible task. When the wisest and most respected had accepted defeat, all others capitulated too.

Only one manager approached the door and gave it a thorough examination. He tapped it, assessed its width and depth, and noticed the nature and lubrication of its hinges. He checked it thoroughly with his eyes and hands. He prodded here, pushed there and poked there. Finally he made his decision. He breathed deeply, centered himself, and pulled gently on the door.

It swung open easily and effortlessly. The others had made the assumption that the door had been locked or jammed. Infact it had been left ever so slightly ajar and the carpentry and design were so excellent that only the slightest touch was required to open it.

The successor had been found. The leader who had gathered them addressed the managers standing before him.

"Success in life and industry depends on certain key attributes. They have just been demonstrated. You must rely on your senses to fully understand the reality of what is going on around you. Furthermore, do not make false assumptions. Thirdly, you must be willing to make difficult decisions. Fourth, have the courage to act with boldness and conviction, and to put your powers into action. Finally, do not be afraid to make mistakes."

Mehdevi, A. S. (1980).

Suggested Reflection and Exercise
1. Personal Reflection:
Think about a time when you assumed a problem was too difficult or impossible without fully investigating it. How did that assumption affect your actions or feelings?

2. Broader Perspective:
Consider how often in life and work people make decisions based on assumptions rather than facts. How might approaching situations with curiosity and openness change outcomes?

3. Questions for Discussion or Writing:
- What assumptions do we commonly make that might limit our success?

- How can we cultivate the courage to act boldly despite uncertainty?

- Why is it important to embrace mistakes as part of learning?

Suggested Practical Activity:

Identify a current challenge or decision you're facing. Take time to observe all details carefully without rushing to conclusions. List any assumptions you might be making and test whether they are true. Then, decide on one bold action to take, accepting that mistakes may happen but are opportunities to learn.

Gandhi's Completeness

People talk of a certain day many years ago, when Gandhi and a companion of his entered the gates of a great city in order to share their teachings with its people. Almost immediately a follower of the Mahatma, who lived in the city, approached and gave him a warning.

"Master, I fear the time you spend here will be fruitless. The people here are hard of heart, they will be unwilling to heed the words of truth. They are ignorant and narrow-minded, with no desire towards the scholarly or spiritual. Do not waste your gifts upon them."

Gandhi smiled at the man and replied, "I have no doubt you are right."

Some minutes later, another follower approached Gandhi, saying, "My lord, you are indeed most welcome by all the people of this fortunate city. We await and anticipate the jewels of learning that will fall from your lips. They are hungry to learn and eager to serve you. Their hearts and minds are truly open to you."

Gandhi smiled and replied once more, "I have no doubt that you too are correct."

His companion queried him, "Master, how is it possible that both men can be correct? The sun and the moon can never be the same thing, and day cannot be night."

Gandhi smiled at his friend and replied, "I have no doubt you are right. And you may also consider that both men spoke truly according to their own views. The first man expects to see the miserable and the imperfect in all things, while the second man sees only the virtuous. Both men see the world as they expect it to be! How can I say that either man is mistaken since all humankind sees the world as they choose to experience it? Neither man spoke falsely, just incompletely."

Owen (2001).

This story beautifully shows how reality is often shaped by our own perspective. Both men spoke the truth, but each saw only part of the whole picture, reflecting their own expectations and beliefs.

Gandhi's response teaches us that:

- Different viewpoints can all hold truths, even if they seem contradictory.

- Our experience of the world is filtered through what we expect or want to see.

- True wisdom comes from recognizing the completeness beyond partial views.

It's a powerful reminder to stay open-minded and humble, appreciating that others' truths might differ but still be valid. What do you think—do you find yourself leaning more toward one viewpoint or appreciating the balance?

Suggested Reflection and Exercise

1. Personal Reflection:

Consider a time when you judged a person or situation quickly based on your own expectations. How might your perspective have been incomplete? How did that affect your feelings or actions?

2. Broader Perspective:

Reflect on how different people can hold valid yet opposing views based on their experiences. How does recognizing this complexity change the way we communicate and coexist?

3. Questions for Discussion or Writing:
- How do your expectations shape your perception of reality?

- Can two conflicting viewpoints both be true at the same time? Why or why not?

- How can embracing incompleteness lead to greater understanding and compassion?

Suggested Practical Activity:

- Active Empathy Practice:

In the coming week, when you encounter a behavior or comment that upsets or frustrates you, pause for a moment before reacting. Ask yourself:

"What might be the other person's perspective or experience that shapes this behavior?"

Try to hold space for multiple truths and observe how this affects your response.

The Food of Paradise

Yunus, the son of Adam, decided one day not only to cast his life upon the balance of fate, but also to seek the reasons for the supply of the particular earthly items gifted to humankind.

"I am," he reasoned to himself, "a man. As such, I get a portion of the world's goods every day. This portion comes to me by my own efforts, coupled with the efforts of others. By simplifying this process, I shall find the means by which food comes to us, and learn how and why. I shall therefore adopt the religious way, which encourages man to rely upon almighty God for his food. Rather than live in the world of confusion, where food and other things come apparently through society, I shall throw myself upon the direct support of the Power that rules over all. The beggar depends upon Good Samaritans: charitable men and women, who are subject to secondary impulses. They give goods or money because they have been brought up to do so. I shall accept no such indirect contributions."

So saying, he walked into the countryside, throwing himself upon the support of invisible forces with the same resolution with which he had accepted the support of visible ones. He fell asleep, certain that Allah would take complete care of his interests, just as the birds and beasts were catered for in their own realm.

At dawn the bird chorus awakened him, and the son of Adam lay still at first, waiting for his food to appear. He maintained his reliance upon the invisible force and his confidence remained intact, certain that he would be able to understand it when it started its operations in the field into which he had thrown himself. Days passed and he sat still, waiting for what was his. His stomach began to grumble louder and louder, he was overcome with an unquenchable thirst. As he sat, he observed packs of wolves feeding together from carrion and, at his very feet, scores of single-minded ants carrying much larger loads on their backs. All the while, he was immobile and growing more famished. He rose to his feet, it dawned on him that speculative thinking alone would not offer much help in this field. So he made his way to the dirt path and wandered to the village he had originally departed from.

Idries Shah (1967).

Suggested Reflection and Exercise

1. Personal Reflection:

Have you ever relied solely on hope or faith without taking action? How did that feel, and what did you learn from that experience? How do you balance trust in a higher power or fate with your own efforts in your daily life?

2. Broader Perspective:

What does this story suggest about the relationship between faith, action, and responsibility? How do different cultures or philosophies address the balance between trusting unseen forces and taking practical steps?

3. Questions for Discussion or Writing:

- Can reliance on faith without action ever be enough? Why or why not?

- How do you interpret the son of Adam's experience with nature (birds, wolves, ants)?

- What role does personal effort play in achieving goals in your life?

Suggested Practical Activity:

- **Balance Reflection:** Over the next week, reflect on areas in your life where you may be relying too much on external factors or faith alone. Identify one small step you can take to actively engage with your goals while maintaining your trust or beliefs. Write down your observations and feelings about this balance.

When the Waters Changed

Once upon a time Khidr, teacher of Moses, called upon mankind with a warning. On a certain date, he cautioned, all the water in the world, which had not been hidden, would evaporate and disappear. It would then be renewed, with different water, which would drive men to madness. Only one man listened to the meaning of this advice. He collected water from every river and lake he could find and went to a secure place where he stored it and waited in apprehension for the water to change.

On the date foretold by Khidr, the streams disappeared, the wells ran dry, and the man who had listened retreated to his sanctuary and drank his preserved water. When he saw the waterfalls beginning to flow once more, this man moved down among the other sons of men. He found that they were thinking and talking in an entirely different way from before; yet they had no memory of what had happened or of the warning given to them. When he tried to talk to them, he realized that they thought him insane; they lashed out fearfully at the man.

At first, he feared the new water and dared not touch it, instead retreating to his inner sanctum to draw on his own supplies each day. Days turned to weeks, and the crushing weight of solitude wore away at his resolve, little by little. One day, he ventured from his place of safety, making his way to a watering hole, he swallowed mouthful after mouthful of the cursed water. He secretly hoped that this would prove the cure to his isolation, that he might behave and think the same as those who had already partaken. He drank the new water, and quickly, his mind changed, becoming like the others. In a moment, he had forgotten all about his own store of water. As he returned amongst his fellow men, they began to look upon him as a madman who, by some miracle, had his sanity returned to him.

Idries Shah (2003).

Suggested Reflection and Exercise

1. Personal Reflection:

Have you ever felt out of sync with others because you saw or understood something differently? How did that affect your relationships or sense of belonging? What does it mean to you to stay true to your convictions even when others don't understand?

2. Broader Perspective:

What might the story say about societal change and how individuals respond to shifting norms or realities? How do we handle the tension between maintaining personal truth and adapting to collective transformation?

3. Questions for Discussion or Writing:

- What does the "water" symbolize in this story?

- Why do you think the man's perspective changed after drinking the new water?

- Can true understanding exist if one loses their unique perspective to fit in?

Suggested Practical Activity:
- **Mindful Observation:** Over the next week, notice moments when your views differ from the majority. Reflect on how you respond—do you conform, resist, or find a balance? Journal about what helps you maintain your integrity while engaging with others.

Elephant in the Dark Room

Five men who had never seen an elephant went into a dark room where an elephant stood. They all felt it with their hands to gain an idea of what it was like. One felt its trunk, and declared that the beast resembled a water-pipe; another felt its ear, and said it must be a large fan; another touched its leg, and thought it must be a pillar; another touched its back, and declared the beast must be like a great throne. According to the part that each touched, he gave a different description of the animal. If each of them held a candle there and if they went in together, they could see it correctly.

(Rumi, Masnavi-e Manavi).

Suggested Reflection and Exercise
1. Personal Reflection:
Recall a situation where you judged something or someone based on limited information. How did that partial view affect your understanding or behavior?

2. Broader Perspective:
This story reminds us how our individual experiences or perspectives can be valid, yet incomplete. In conflict, teamwork, or social issues, how often do people argue over "truth" when they are simply seeing different parts of the whole?

3. Questions for Discussion or Writing:
- What helps people become more open to perspectives other than their own?

- How can group decision-making benefit from recognizing partial views?

- In what areas of your life could more collaboration or shared insight bring clarity?

Suggested Practical Activity:

Choose a topic you feel strongly about. Then, actively seek out three different perspectives on the same issue (from articles, conversations, or media). Write a paragraph summarizing what each viewpoint adds to the bigger picture. Reflect on what changed in your understanding.

How We Entrapped Ourselves?

In the canopy of a vast forest there dwelt a monkey who, above all other earthly things, adored cherries. On one afternoon, from his vantage point high in the trees, he spotted a ripe cherry on its lonesome right beneath. He came bounding down his tree to collect the scrumptious treat. But, as he anxiously reached for the fruit, his hand was met with a clink and a sharp pain. He looked down to see a glass bottle surrounding the cherry. After some experimentation, the monkey found that he could get hold of the cherry by putting his hand through the bottle's neck. As soon as he had done so, he closed his hand over the cherry; but then he discovered that his fist was too wide to pull out while he held the cherry.

Unbeknownst to the monkey, this was very much deliberate, the cherry in the bottle was a trap laid by a hunter who knew of monkeys' irrational love of sweet things. The hunter, hearing shrieks and cries of frustration, came to investigate his trap. The monkey heard the rustling of the shrubs nearby and tried to escape. But, because his hand was stuck in the heavy bottle, he could not move fast enough to escape the man. The monkey, of course, still gripped the cherry tightly. The hunter picked him up. A moment later he tapped the monkey sharply on the elbow, eliciting a screech and the unconscious release of the fruit. The monkey was free of the bottle, but found himself in the arms of his captor. The cherry that the monkey had been so unwilling to relinquish was now back in the trapper's hand.

De Vos (2003).

Suggested Reflection and Exercise
1. Personal Reflection:
Think about a time when you held on to something—even when it was causing you harm or holding you back. What made it hard to let go? How did holding on affect you?

2. Broader Perspective:
This story highlights how attachments, even to small desires or fears, can trap us. How might this apply to people's behavior in everyday life, relationships, or work? What can it teach us about flexibility and letting go?

3. Questions for Discussion or Writing:
- Why do you think the monkey refused to let go of the cherry, even though it was caught?

- What are some "cherries" in your life—things you cling to that might limit your freedom or happiness?

- How can awareness of this tendency help us make better choices?

Suggested Practical Activity:
- **Letting Go Practice:** Over the next few days, notice moments when you feel attached to a particular outcome, possession, or belief. Pause and ask yourself, "Is holding on helping me or hurting me?" Try gently relaxing your grip—whether literally or mentally—and observe what happens.

Namouss the Shrewd

Once upon a time there was a gnat by the name of Namouss. He was known, because of his observant nature, as Namouss the Shrewd. Namouss decided, after much reflection upon his current lifestyle, to find himself a new home. The place which he chose as very suitable was the ear of a certain elephant.

All that remained to do was to make the move, and quite soon, Namouss had installed himself in the spacious residence. Time passed. The gnat cared for several families of young gnats, and he sent them out into the world. As years came and went, he knew the usual moments of anxiety and calm, the feelings of joy and sorrow, of questing and achievement, which are the lot of the gnat wherever he may be found.

The elephant's ear was his home and, as is always the case, he felt that there was a close connection between his life, his history—indeed his very being—and this place. The ear was boundless, warm and familiar: the scene of so many experiences.

Naturally, Namouss had not moved into the house without due ceremony or due regard for the proper observances of the occasion. On the very first day, just before moving in, he had cried out, at the top of his tiny lungs, his decision.

"Oh elephant," he had cried, "Know that none other than I, Namouss the gnat, Namouss the Shrewd, propose to make this place my home! As it is your ear, I am giving you the customary notice of my intention."

The elephant had raised no objection.

But, Namouss did not know that the elephant had not heard him at all. Neither, for that matter, had his host felt the entry (or even the presence and absence of the gnat and his various families). He had no idea that gnats were there at all. And when the time came, Namouss the Shrewd decided that he would move home again, he reflected that he must do so in accordance with his established and hallowed custom. He prepared himself for the formal declaration of his abandonment of the elephant's ear.

Thus, it was finally and forever decided, and when his words were sufficiently rehearsed, Namouss shouted once more down the elephant's ear. He shouted once, and no answer came. He shouted again, and the elephant was still silent. The third time, gathering the whole strength of his voice in his determination to register his urgent yet powerful words, he cried out. "Oh elephant! Know that I, the gnat, Shrewd Namouss, propose to leave my home, to abandon my residence in your ear in which I have stayed for so very long. And this is for a sufficient and significant reason which I am prepared to explain to you."

Now finally the words of the mosquito came to the hearing of the elephant, and the gnat's cry penetrated.

As the elephant pondered the words, Namouss shouted, "What have you to say in answer to my news? What are your feelings about my departure?"

The elephant raised his great head and trumpeted a little.

This trumpeting contained the sentiment, "Go in peace—for in truth your going is of as much interest and significance to me as was your coming."

Idries Shah (1967).

Suggested Reflection and Exercise

1. Personal Reflection:

Have you ever put great effort into informing or impacting someone who seemed unaware or indifferent? How did that make you feel? Can you relate to Namouss's experience of being unnoticed despite your intentions?

2. Broader Perspective:

What does this story suggest about the importance of perspective and awareness in communication? How might it apply to relationships, work, or society when some voices go unheard?

3. Questions for Discussion or Writing:

- Why do you think Namouss felt the need to announce his arrival and departure so formally?

- What might the elephant's response say about the significance of small events to larger beings or systems?

- How can we be more mindful about truly listening and noticing those around us?

Suggested Practical Activity:
- **Active Awareness Practice:** In the coming days, choose one person or situation where you usually feel unheard or unnoticed. Make a conscious effort to express yourself clearly, and observe both how you communicate and how others respond. Reflect on any changes in understanding or connection.

The Man Who Sold His House and Cat

A man, facing personal troubles, vows that if his problems are resolved, he will sell his house and donate all the proceeds to the poor. Once his situation improves, he becomes reluctant to part with the money. To circumvent his oath, he sells his house for a nominal sum (e.g., one silver coin) but includes a cat priced exorbitantly (e.g., ten thousand silver coins). He donates the small amount from the house sale and keeps the larger sum from the cat's sale, technically fulfilling his vow but violating its spirit.

This story serves as a cautionary tale about the dangers of legalism and the importance of integrity. It highlights how individuals might manipulate technicalities to avoid genuine moral obligations. Many people's minds work in such a way. They decide to follow a teaching but they interpret it only to their own advantage. Until they overcome this tendency, many find it difficult to learn at all.

(Jewish Folklore).

Suggested Reflection and Exercise
1. Personal Reflection:

Have you ever made a promise or commitment but later found it difficult to keep? How did you handle the conflict between your intentions and your actions?

2. Broader Perspective:

What does this story reveal about human nature and the challenges of integrity? How might selective interpretation of principles affect personal growth and relationships?

3. Questions for Discussion or Writing:

- Why do you think the man chose to manipulate his promise instead of fulfilling it honestly?

- How can people guard against self-deception when making commitments?

- What are the consequences of bending ethical rules for personal gain?

Suggested Practical Activity:
- **Integrity Check:** Reflect on a recent commitment you made. Are there any ways you've been tempted to rationalize or avoid it? Write down one small step you can take to honor that commitment more fully this week.

Losing Yourself

There are many ways to wake up, but only one right way. It doesn't matter how you sleep—but how you wake up does.

Once, a foolish man came to a big, crowded city. He saw so many people and thought, "If I go to sleep, how will I know who I am when I wake up?" So he tied a rope around his own ankle to recognize himself later.

While he was sleeping, a man who liked to play tricks noticed the rope. He untied it from the fool's leg and tied it to his own leg, then lay down nearby and went to sleep too.

When the fool woke up and saw the rope on the other man's leg, he panicked. He shook the man and shouted, "If you are me, then who am I and where did I go?"

Salahi (2002).

Suggested Reflection and Exercise

1. Personal Reflection:

Have you ever felt confused about your own identity or purpose, especially after a major change or new experience? How did you find clarity?

2. Broader Perspective:

What does this story suggest about the importance of self-awareness and understanding in our lives? How can confusion about who we are affect our actions and relationships?

3. Questions for Discussion or Writing:

- Why did the fool tie the rope around his ankle, and what does this symbolize?

- How does the prank played by the joker deepen the fool's confusion?

- What might "awakening the right way" look like in real life?

Suggested Practical Activity:
- **Mindful Self-Check:** Spend five minutes each morning reflecting on who you are beyond external labels or roles. Write down one thing you discover about yourself that is constant, regardless of your situation.

How a Tradition Was Born

There was once a town made up of two streets that ran side by side. One day, a traveler walked along one street and then into the other. When he reached the second street, people saw that his eyes were full of tears.

Someone shouted, "Someone must have died in the other street!" Soon, all the children began to cry too. The traveler was confused—he had only been peeling onions.

Within minutes, the crying spread to the first street. But no one knew what had caused all the sadness. The adults became scared and didn't want to investigate. A wise man tried to help, asking why they didn't just talk to each other. But people were afraid. Some thought there might be a deadly disease in the other street, so no one dared to go.

The rumor of danger spread quickly. Each street believed the other was in serious trouble. In the end, both communities decided to leave to protect themselves.

Years later, the old town was empty, and two villages now existed nearby. Each village told the story of how they left a doomed town long ago to escape some mysterious danger. And that's how a tradition—and a misunderstanding—were born.

Coelho (2007).

Suggested Reflection and Exercise
1. Personal Reflection:
Can you recall a time when a misunderstanding or rumor caused unnecessary fear or conflict in your life or community? How did it affect your relationships or decisions?

2. Broader Perspective:
What does this story tell us about the power of assumptions and communication in shaping traditions, beliefs, or even history? How can false stories or fear influence group behavior?

3. Questions for Discussion or Writing:
- How did the seeker's innocent action lead to a chain of misunderstandings?

- Why were the people so quick to believe in a deadly plague without verifying?

- How can communities avoid falling into such patterns of fear and division?

Suggested Practical Activity:
- **Pause and Verify:** When you hear alarming news or rumors, take a moment before reacting. Seek to verify the facts and consider different perspectives before sharing or acting on the information.

The Bird and the Egg

A bird lived in a large wilderness. Unlike other birds that could fly high in the sky, this bird couldn't fly at all. He always watched the others soar above him while he walked on the ground.

One day, by chance, he found an egg that had been left behind. He decided to take care of it. After many days of keeping it warm, the egg finally hatched. A chick came out, and right away, it looked different—its feathers and wings showed it was a bird meant to fly.

The chick asked, "When will I learn how to fly, Father?"

The bird who raised him said, "If you keep trying, someday you'll fly like the others."

But the ground bird didn't really know how to teach him flying—he didn't even know how to start. Still, the young bird was grateful. "Without him, I would never have hatched," he thought.

Time passed, and even though the chick grew strong wings, he never left the ground. He still believed, "One day, the one who raised me will teach me how to fly. He helped me this far—he'll help me with the rest too."

Idries Shah (1967).

Suggested Reflection and Exercise

1. Personal Reflection:

Have you ever relied on someone's help or guidance, expecting them to teach or support you, only to realize they couldn't provide what you needed? How did that affect your growth or independence?

2. Broader Perspective:

What does this story suggest about the limits of care and the importance of self-reliance? How might expectations of others hold us back from taking initiative?

3. Questions for Discussion or Writing:

- Why did the young bird believe the adopter would eventually teach it to fly?

- How can waiting for others to guide us sometimes prevent our own progress?

- What is the balance between receiving support and taking personal responsibility for growth?

Suggested Practical Activity:
- **Take Initiative Challenge:** Identify one area in your life where you are waiting for guidance or support. This week, take one small step on your own to advance without waiting for external help.

Logic Isn't Always Enough

A smart and curious man was traveling when he came across a small village. Wanting to understand different opinions, he went to a local restaurant and asked, "Who is the most honest person here, and who is the biggest liar?"

The villagers told him, "Siddiq is the honest one. Dolos is the liar."

The man visited both and asked each of them the same question, "What's the best way to get to the next village?"

Both said, "Take the mountain path."

This confused the traveler. Why would both the honest man and the liar say the same thing?

He asked a few more villagers. Some said to go by the river, others said across the fields.

In the end, he took the mountain path and reached the next village without trouble. But the question still bothered him. So he told his story at a rest house[1].

He said, "I must have asked the wrong people. I thought I was talking to an honest man and a liar, but they gave me the same answer."

1- Roadside inn

A wise man there replied, "You didn't ask the wrong people. You just missed something important. The liar said "mountain path' because the easiest way was the river—and he wanted to mislead you. But the honest man noticed you had a donkey. With a donkey, the mountain path is just fine. The liar didn't see that you had no boat, or he would've sent you to the river to confuse you. It's not just about truth or lies—observation matters too."

Mehdevi, A. S. (1980).

Suggested Reflection and Exercise
1. Personal Reflection:

Have you ever encountered a situation where two opposing viewpoints both seemed true? How did you decide which to trust? How did your own circumstances shape that decision?

2. Broader Perspective:

What does this story reveal about truth, perspective, and context? How can rigid assumptions about truth limit our understanding?

3. Questions for Discussion or Writing:

- Why did both the truthful man and the liar give the same answer?

- How does context influence what we consider true or false?

- What role does observation play in discerning deeper truths beyond words?

Suggested Practical Activity:
- **Context Awareness Practice:** This week, when you hear conflicting opinions, try to explore the context behind each one before forming a judgment. Reflect on how circumstances might influence each viewpoint.

"Two Paths, One Life"

There was a man named Adi, the Calculator, known for his skills in math. One day, he decided to leave his hometown of Bukhara to search for deeper knowledge. Before he left, his teacher gave him some advice:

"Head south," the teacher said, "and try to understand the meaning behind the peacock and the snake."

Adi thought deeply about his teacher's advice as he traveled through Khorasan and eventually reached Iraq. To his surprise, he actually saw a peacock and a snake facing each other. Curious and excited, he approached them and asked what they were doing.

"We're having a conversation," said the peacock, "about which one of us is more important."

"This is exactly what I came to learn about!" Adi said. "Please, go on!"

The peacock started, "I believe I'm more important. People see me as a symbol of high hopes, spiritual beauty, and rising toward the heavens. I represent the higher knowledge and remind humans of the deeper, hidden parts of themselves."

Then the snake spoke, "But I stand for the physical world. Like humans, I stay close to the Earth. People forget how much we have in common. We're both flexible and able to adapt to life's challenges. Plus, I'm the one who protects the treasures buried deep in the earth."

"But you're disgusting," said the peacock. "You're sneaky, secretive, and dangerous!"

The snake calmly replied, "You're judging me just by how I look. I prefer to see what's underneath the surface. Look at yourself—you're full of pride for being a fat bird with silly feathers and an annoying voice."

Adi, who had been quietly listening all along, finally spoke up. "I can see that neither of you is completely right. But if we set aside your personal attacks, there's a clear message for humanity in the differences between you."

Then, while both the peacock and the snake listened, Adi began to explain what each of them truly represented.

"Humans live close to the ground like the snake," Adi said. "But they also have the potential to rise high like a bird. Yet when humans try to rise, they often bring their selfishness with them, just like the snake. And then, they become like the peacock—proud and showy. The peacock represents what humans could become, but in the wrong way—flashy instead of truly elevated."

Then a voice from deep inside Adi spoke:

"That's not the full picture. Both the snake and the peacock are alive—and that's what matters most. They fight because each has chosen only one way of being and believes it's the perfect life. But look deeper: the snake protects treasure underground but can't use it. The peacock shows off beauty—a kind of treasure—but can't grow or change through it. Even though they haven't made the most of their potential, they still symbolize it—for those wise enough to see and understand."

Mehdevi, A. S. (1980).

Suggested Reflection and Exercise
1. Personal Reflection:

Think about a time when you acted more like the snake—practical, grounded, focused on what's tangible. How did this affect your decisions and growth? Then, think of a time when you acted more like the peacock—proud, reaching for higher ideals or showing off. What were the results? How do these two sides show up in your life?

2. Broader Perspective:

Consider how people or societies sometimes focus only on material success (snake) or on appearance and status (peacock). What problems can arise when one side dominates? How can balancing both roundedness and aspiration improve personal and social well-being?

3. Questions for Discussion or Writing:
- Which qualities of the snake and peacock do you admire, and which do you find challenging?

- How can pride become a barrier rather than a strength?

- What does it mean to fully use your "treasures" or gifts rather than just symbolize them?

Suggested Practical Activity:
- Appreciation Journal: For one week, write daily entries about moments when you acted like the snake (practical, grounded) and moments when you acted like the peacock (aspirational, proud). Reflect on what you learned about yourself from balancing these two parts.

The Water of Paradise

Once upon a time, there was a desert Arab man who had spent his whole life in the sandy desert with his family. He had never seen a city.

They lived in their tent near a small stream that came from the bottom of a hill and disappeared into the sand. They mostly ate desert plants, locusts, and things like that.

By the spring of water, there was an old tree that had no fruit. From far away, it looked green, but up close, it looked burnt. The spring water was salty, and in summer, it became so low that it was only enough to quench their thirst.

The Arab man had always thought that place was his home, and he didn't know if there was a better place in the world. When someone has never seen a better life, they get used to what they have and don't expect much. The man thought that if he left, someone else would take over their home.

When life got very hard, he would go to the caravan route far away and wait a long time, hoping a caravan would pass by, so he could get some charity and news. But caravans came very rarely.

One year, there was a drought. The salty spring water became less and less until it almost dried up. No matter how much they dug the damp ground, there was no more water to be found.

One day, while walking in the desert, he found a spring he had never seen before. The water was very clear. He drank some and was amazed—it tasted better than anything he had ever tried. He thought it must be the "water of paradise."

Feeling excited, he wanted to share the water with someone important. So, he put some water in a container and began a long journey to Baghdad, where the King lived. After many weeks of travel, he finally reached the palace and asked to see the King.

When he met the King, he said, "I am just a poor man, but I found what I believe is water from paradise. I brought some as a gift for you."

The King tasted the water, but to him, it was bitter and tasted bad! Still, he did not laugh or insult Harith. Instead, he was kind. He told a guard, "What seems useless to us is very precious to this man. Take him back to his spring, but don't let him see the big, beautiful Tigris River. Give him 1,000 gold coins and ask him to offer his water to travelers in my name."

Yazdi Azar (1968).

Suggested Reflection and Exercise
1. Personal Reflection:
Have you ever experienced something deeply meaningful or valuable that others didn't understand or appreciate? How did that affect your view of yourself and your experience?

2. Broader Perspective:
What does this story suggest about the difference between personal values and collective or societal values? How can understanding this help us respect different perspectives?

3. Questions for Discussion or Writing:
- Why did the King reject the water that was so precious to the man?

- How might the King's power and wealth shape his perception of what is valuable?

- What does this story say about the relationship between experience and understanding?

Suggested Practical Activity:
- **Appreciation Journal:** Take a moment each day to note something meaningful or beautiful to you, regardless of whether others recognize its value. Reflect on why it matters personally.

Jesus and the Doubters

The master, Jalāludin Rumi, relates the tale of Jesus, the son of Maryam, who one day was traversing the desert near Jerusalem with a group of covetous people who sought his invaluable knowledge.

Many begged Jesus for the secret name that would return the dead to the realm of the living. They would claim arrogantly that they were ready and deserving of such knowledge and that it would strengthen their faith. He chided them.

"You do not know what you ask," he said.

But he gave them the word they so desired nonetheless. Soon afterwards, as the people walked back through the desert, they stumbled upon a heap of whitened bones. Anxious to test the word of power Jesus had gifted them that they spoke the word. No sooner than the words had formed on their lips, the inanimate pile of bones rearranged and wrapped itselves in flesh. Standing before them stood a ravenous wild beast unlike anything they had ever behold, it stared at them with its feral and nightmarish gaze. Then, in a moment, it leapt upon them, tearing each and every man and woman apart in a wild frenzy. Those endowed with reason will understand this cautionary account, and those without reason might learn it if they study the tale for long enough.

(Rumi, Masnavi-e Manavi).

Suggested Reflection and Exercise

1. Personal Reflection:

Have you ever wanted something—knowledge, power, or certainty—before you felt truly ready for it? How did that desire affect your choices or understanding?

2. Broader Perspective:

What does this story teach about the responsibility that comes with knowledge or power? How might premature or careless use of knowledge bring harm?

3. Questions for Discussion or Writing:

- Why do you think Jesus warned the people they didn't know what they asked for?

- What might the wild beast symbolize in the story?

- How can wisdom and readiness be cultivated before seeking or using powerful knowledge?

Suggested Practical Activity:
- **Mindful Learning:** Before rushing to gain new knowledge or skills, pause and ask yourself: Am I truly ready to use this wisely? Reflect on how preparation changes your understanding.

The Parable of Greedy Sons

There was an industrious and charitable farmer, who had at his side a number of listless and greedy sons. As he lay dying, he whispered to his sons that they would find his treasure buried in a certain field. The moment he drew his last breath, his sons hurried out into the field to search for the promised bounty. They dug up the farm from one end to another, digging until they reached bedrock, their desperation growing with each failed attempt at locating the bounty.

No matter how deep or how distant the holes that they dug were, they found nothing. They realized that their father, in his generosity, had donated the gold while he was alive and abandoned their search. It occurred to them that they might as well use the land they dug up to sow the wheat seeds their father had left behind to make up for their lost time and effort. The wheat produced an abundant yield, which they sold for great profit.

After selling the wheat, they once more dug up the fields, in the hope that somehow they had missed the stash of hidden gold. The result was the same as before. So, accepting that the treasure could not be found, they used a fraction of their earlier profits to buy seeds to plant in the tilled earth. After several seasons of this, they became accustomed to the hard labor of sowing and harvesting. It occurred to them, one by one, that this had been their father's intention all along. After years of this menial work, the sons discovered that they had accrued enough wealth to never have to worry about the supposed hidden hoard again.

This is how it is with the teaching of the destiny of people. The teacher, faced with impatience, selfishness and greed amongst his pupils, must direct them such that they feel they satisfy their own self-interest, but have in fact been orchestrated to fulfill a greater role.

Berman, M. & Brown, D. (2000).

Suggested Reflection and Exercise

1. Personal Reflection:

Have you ever pursued something with impatience or greed, only to realize that the true reward was in the process or journey itself? How do you balance desire for quick results with patience for gradual growth?

2. Broader Perspective:

What does this story suggest about the role of effort and perseverance in achieving lasting success or wisdom? How might impatience or selfishness blind us to deeper lessons?

3. Questions for Discussion or Writing:

- Why did the father send his sons on a seemingly fruitless search?

- How did the sons' attitudes change over time?

- What can this teach us about the way knowledge or spiritual growth is imparted?

Suggested Practical Activity:
- **Patience Practice:** Choose a goal or project that requires sustained effort. Commit to working on it with patience for a set period (a week, a month). At the end, reflect on what you learned through the process beyond the results.

Hot Buttons

Mole was driving along the motorway with his friend, Badger. Mole was enjoying the scenic drive, feeling good about the world. That was until another car, driven by Rat, aggressively and dangerously cut him up.

Mole was irate. He slammed the accelerator and chased after Rat, veins on his forehead pulsing, gripping the wheel so tightly his knuckles had turned white. Mole was shouting and cursing, as he sped up. Ahead of them, Rat simply laughed to himself, made a rude gesture and accelerated away.

Mole sat in a brooding silence for the next hour. His day was totally spoilt. He felt frustrated and inadequate—as if his whole sense of masculinity had been called into question. He had been challenged and come off second best. Badger had noticed his friend's behavior but had chosen to say nothing for the time being. He waited until the time was right. Finally, Mole turned to him and said, "That sort of driver makes me so angry."

Badger replied, "Forgive me, but I'm really curious. How exactly do you allow yourself to get angry because of what another driver does?"

Mole was speechless; he had expected support.

"What do you mean?"

(Anonymous).

Suggested Reflection and Exercise
1. Personal Reflection:
Think of a time when someone's actions triggered a strong emotional reaction in you, especially anger or frustration. What part of your identity or values did you feel was threatened or challenged? What might have happened if you had paused before reacting?

2. Broader Perspective:
Consider how often we give others the power to control our emotions, especially strangers or minor incidents. What does this suggest about emotional maturity and self-awareness in daily life? What do we teach others—especially children— through how we respond?

3. Questions for Discussion or Writing:
- Is anger always a reaction to others, or can it also be rooted in something internal?

- What role does ego or pride play in emotional reactivity?

- How can we build emotional resilience in situations that provoke us?

4. Suggested Practical Activity:

Over the next few days, observe your emotional reactions, especially anger or irritation. When you notice yourself reacting, pause and ask, "Am I giving someone else control over my emotions?" Write down any patterns you notice and reflect on how you might respond differently next time.

Jesus Escaping from Fools

Jesus, the son of Mary, was running quickly toward a mountain, as if a lion were chasing him to kill him. A man saw him and ran after him, shouting, "Why are you running like a bird? No one is chasing you!"

But Jesus kept running so fast that he didn't even hear the man. The man kept following and calling out, "For God's sake, stop a moment and tell me why you're running. There's no enemy, no lion, nothing threatening you. Why such hurry?"

Jesus finally said, "Don't follow me. I'm running away from a fool—I'm trying to save myself."

The man said, "Aren't you the same Jesus who heals the blind and the deaf?"

Jesus replied, "Yes, I am."

The man asked, "Aren't you the prophet who knows hidden things and can bring the dead back to life just by speaking to them?"

Jesus said, "Yes, that's me."

The man continued, "Aren't you the one who can shape a bird out of clay and give it life?"

Jesus said, "Yes."

The man said, "O pure soul! With such powers, who wouldn't follow and respect you?"

Jesus replied, "By God, everything you see in this world is created by him. I used the Greatest Name of God to heal the blind and deaf, and they were cured. I spoke it to a mountain, and it crumbled. I used it on the dead, and they came back to life. But I have read it to fools thousands of times—and nothing happened. They didn't change."

The man then asked, "Why did it work before, but not now? Aren't both blindness and foolishness kinds of suffering?"

Jesus said, "The suffering of foolishness is a punishment from God. But blindness and deafness are tests—trials that can lead to God's mercy and forgiveness. Foolishness, on the other hand, brings harm to both oneself and others."

(Rumi, Masnavu-e Manavi).

Suggested Reflection and Exercise
1. Personal Reflection:

- Have you ever found yourself surrounded by people who refused to understand, listen, or grow—no matter how much you tried?

- How did that make you feel? What did you do in that situation?

- Are there moments when you might have been closed off to understanding or wisdom from others?

2. Broader Perspective:

- What is the story saying about the difference between physical limitations (like blindness or deafness) and ignorance?

- Why is ignorance portrayed as more dangerous and unchangeable than other struggles?

- What does this story teach about the limits of even great wisdom or power when met with unwillingness?

3. Questions for Discussion or Writing:

- Why do you think Jesus fled from fools but helped the blind and deaf?

- What does this teach us about where to invest our energy and care?

- How can we recognize when we're dealing with foolishness, not just disagreement?

Suggested Practical Activity:

- Awareness Journal:

For one week, reflect daily on conversations or interactions where you tried to share or help.

Ask yourself:
- Was the other person open or closed to growth?

The Fool and the Browsing Camel

A camel browsing a store noticed an idiot gawking at him. The idiot asked, "You are such a misshapen and irregular creature! Why is this so?"

The camel retorted, "In judging me with your first glimpse do you not see that you attribute fault to He who shaped my form? Do not consider my crooked appearance a defect!"

"Leave my presence as quickly as you can," the camel continued, "My exterior is as it was created for a reason, the bow needs the crookedness of the wood as well as the straightness of the bowstring. Begone! An ass's perception goes with an ass's nature

(Rumi, Masnavi-e Manavi).

Suggested Reflection and Exercise

1. Personal Reflection:

Have you ever judged someone or something quickly, based only on appearances? How did that affect your understanding or relationship with them?

2. Broader Perspective:

What does the camel's response teach about the nature of imperfections or differences? How might flaws or irregularities have a purpose beyond what we immediately see?

3. Questions for Discussion or Writing:

- Why does the camel compare itself to a bow?

- What does the story suggest about the way we should view "imperfections" in ourselves or others?

- How does this story challenge common assumptions about beauty or normalcy?

Suggested Practical Activity:
- **Mindful Observation:** Next time you catch yourself making a quick judgment, pause and consider what purpose or value the "imperfection" might have. Write down your thoughts or discuss with someone.

Three Jeweled Rings

There was once a clever and affluent man who lived with his son. He said to him, "My son, here is a jeweled ring. Keep it as a sign that you are a successor of mine and pass it down to your posterity. It is very valuable, very beautiful, and it has the helpful capacity of opening a certain door to wealth."

Some years later he had another son. When he was old enough, the wise man gave him another ring, with the same advice. The same thing happened once more in the case of his third and last son.

When the father had died and the sons had grown up, one after the other, each claimed primacy for himself because of his possession of one of the rings. Nobody could tell for certain which was the most valuable. Each son gained his adherents, all claiming a greater value or beauty for his own ring. But the curious thing was that the "door to wealth" remained shut for the possessors of the keys and even their closest supporters. They were all too preoccupied with the problem of precedence, the possession of the ring, its value and appearance.

Only a few looked for the door to the treasury of the ring maker. But the rings had a magical quality, too. Although they were keys, they were not used directly in opening the door to the treasury. It was sufficient to look upon them without contention or too much attachment to one or the other of their qualities. When this had been done, the people who had looked were able to tell where the treasury was and could open it merely by reproducing the outline of the ring. The treasuries had another quality, too: they were inexhaustible.

Meanwhile, the partisans of the three rings repeated the tale of their ancestor about the merits of the rings, each in a slightly different way.

Lessing, Gotthold Ephraim (1986).

Suggested Reflection and Exercise

1. Personal Reflection:

Have you ever been caught up in competition or comparison with others over something symbolic—like status, possessions, or titles—while missing the deeper meaning or purpose behind it?

2. Broader Perspective:

What might the "rings" represent beyond their physical form? How does the story suggest we should relate to symbols of value or power?

3. Questions for Discussion or Writing:

- Why do you think the sons were unable to open the door despite having the rings?

- What does the story imply about attachment to external signs versus seeking the source or essence?

- How can looking "without contention or too much attachment" change our understanding or experience?

Suggested Practical Activity:

- Contemplative Practice:

Think about something you highly value or compete for in your life. Reflect on its true purpose or meaning. Consider how detaching from competition or pride around it might reveal deeper benefits or insights.

The Illusion of Devotion

One day, a man came to Bayazid Bastami, the great mystic, to share his concerns. He said that he had been fasting, praying, and showing kindness to others for thirty years, but he had not yet found the joy and pleasure that Bayazid had promised.

Bayazid replied, "Even if you continue these practices for three hundred more years, you may still not reach that joy. The problem lies within yourself, not in your outward actions."

He added, "When you count your deeds by calculation, you are not truly doing the right work. Change your attitude and expectations to find happiness."

Mehdevi, A. S. (1980).

Suggested Reflection and Exercise
1. Personal Reflection:
- Think about times when you've focused more on the results of your actions rather than the sincerity behind them. How did that affect your feelings and motivation?

- Have you ever practiced kindness or discipline expecting a reward or recognition? How did that impact your experience?

2. Broader Perspective:
- Consider how genuine intention might be more important than outward actions in any spiritual or personal growth. How does this idea apply to relationships or work in your life?

- Reflect on the difference between performing actions mechanically and engaging with full awareness and sincerity.

3. Questions for Discussion or Writing:

- Why do you think Bayazid said the problem was within the man's self and not in his actions?

- How can we practice kindness or discipline without attaching ourselves to the outcomes?

- In what ways can focusing too much on results hinder true growth or happiness?

Suggested Practical Activity:

- Mindful Action Practice: For one day, pick one routine activity (e.g., eating, walking, or helping someone). Do it with full attention and without expecting any reward or recognition. Afterwards, reflect on how this felt compared to doing it with an expectation of outcome.

Who Attain

Jesus one day saw some people sitting miserably on a wall by the roadside.

He asked, "What is your affliction?"

They replied, "We have become like this due to our fear of hell."

He went on his way and saw a number of people grouped dejectedly by the wayside. Again, he asked, "What is your affliction?"

These people replied, "The desire for Paradise has made us this way."

He went on his way until he came to a third group of people.

They looked like people who had endured much, but still their faces shone with joy.

Jesus asked them, "What has made you like this?"

They responded, "The Spirit of Truth. We have seen Reality, and this has made us oblivious of lesser goals"

Jesus mused, "These are the people who attain. One day they will be in the presence of God."

Idries Shah (1971).

Suggested Reflection and Exercise

1. Personal Reflection:

Which of the three groups do you most resonate with right now—the fearful, the desirous, or the joyful with "lesser goals"? What might "lesser goals" mean in your own life?

2. Broader Perspective:

Why do you think Jesus points to those with "the spirit of lesser goals" as the ones who truly attain? How can focusing on smaller, immediate steps lead to deeper fulfillment or spiritual presence?

3. Questions for Discussion or Writing:

- How can fear of hell or desire for paradise affect one's mindset and actions?

- What is the value of contentment or joy in everyday, small achievements?

- How might shifting your focus from grand outcomes to "lesser goals" change your experience of life and growth?

Suggested Practical Activity:

- Set a Lesser Goal:

Choose a simple, attainable goal for this week—something smaller than your usual ambitions. Notice how pursuing it affects your sense of progress, peace, or joy.

Noticing Your Way to Freedom

A man in prison was sent a prayer rug by his friend. What he had wanted, of course, was a file or a crowbar or a key! But he began using the rug, doing the five-times daily prayers before dawn, at noon, mid-afternoon, after sunset, and before sleep. Bowing, sitting up, bowing again, he noticed an odd pattern in the weave of the rug, just at the *qibla,* the point, where his head touches. He studied and meditated on that pattern, gradually discovering that it was a diagram of the lock that confines him in his cell and how it works. He was able to escape. ***Anything you do every day can open into the deepest spiritual place, which is freedom.***

CONSIDER THIS: Anything you do every day can open into the deepest spiritual place, which is freedom.

Barks, C. (2004).

Suggested Reflection and Exercise

1. Personal Reflection:

- Have you ever been in a situation where something simple or unexpected helped you see things differently or solve a problem?

- What daily habit or routine do you do that could hold hidden meaning or offer a deeper insight?

2. Broader Perspective:

- This story reminds us that spiritual awareness can come not just from dramatic changes, but through consistent, mindful practice.

- How might regular discipline, patience, and attention to detail lead to breakthroughs in difficult or "locked" parts of our lives?

3. Questions for Discussion or Writing:

- What is the difference between looking and noticing?

- How can attending rituals (prayer, meditation, or any repeated act), become a way to freedom or growth?

- What does this story suggest about the value of persistence in confined or limiting situations?

Suggested Practical Activity

- Appreciation Journal:

The Literature Teacher in the Well

One dark night, Nasreddin was walking past a dry well when he heard someone shouting for help from inside.

"What's going on?" he called down.

"I'm a literature teacher," came the reply. "And unfortunately, I fell into this deep well because I didn't watch my step. Now I can't get out!"

"Hold on, my friend," said Nasreddin. "I'll go get a ladder and a rope to pull you out."

"Wait a minute," said the teacher. "You mispronounced ladder and rope, and your grammar could use some work. Please correct it before continuing."

Nasreddin shouted back, "Well, if fixing my grammar is more important than getting you out, you might as well stay there until I've learned to speak properly!" Then he walked away.

Salahi (2002).

Suggested Reflection and Exercise
1. Personal Reflection:
- Have you ever focused too much on small details and missed the bigger picture?

- Can you recall a time when pride or perfectionism stopped you from receiving or giving help?

2. Broader Perspective:
- This story highlights how prioritizing form over function can lead to missed opportunities.

- In education, relationships, or even activism, do we sometimes value being "right" over being helpful or kind?

- What are the dangers of intellectual arrogance in real-life situations?

3. Questions for Discussion or Writing:

- What is the main lesson Nasreddin is teaching through his reaction?

- Who is wiser in this story—the teacher or Nasreddin? Why?

- How might this story apply to communication in our modern digital age?

Suggested Practical Activity:

- Listening Practice Journal:

Keep a journal for one week where you reflect daily on your conversations. Note if you listened more to understand or to correct. Identify one moment each day when you chose kindness or practicality over being "right."

Nasruddin and the princess

Once there was a princess who was incredibly beautiful—everyone who saw her couldn't help but admire her. One day, Nasruddin was about to eat some bread when he caught sight of her walking by. He was so stunned by her beauty that the bread slipped from his hand and fell to the ground.

As she passed, the princess gave him a gentle smile. That simple gesture made Nasruddin completely lose control—he was so overwhelmed he could barely think straight. From that day on, he stayed in the same spot on the street for seven whole years, sleeping next to stray dogs, hoping he might see her again. Nasruddin became a problem for the princess, and her helpers thought it was best to get rid of him. But the princess called him over and said, "We can never be together. My servants want to kill you, so you need to leave."

Feeling sad, Nasruddin said, "Since I saw you, life has lost its meaning. If they want to kill me, I won't fight. But please, before that happens, tell me—why did you smile at me in the first place?"

The princess laughed and said, "You silly man! I smiled because I felt sorry for how foolish you were acting. That's all." Then she walked away and was gone.

Salahi (2002).

Suggested Reflection and Exercise
1. Personal Reflection:
Have you ever been so captivated or obsessed with something or someone that it affected your sense of self or well-being? How did that experience shape your understanding of attachment and desire?

2. Broader Perspective:
What does this story reveal about the nature of infatuation, illusion, and the dangers of losing oneself in unreciprocated feelings? How might this relate to spiritual longing versus worldly desires?

3. Questions for Discussion or Writing:
- How does the seeker's reaction to the princess's smile illustrate the power of perception and projection?

- What might the princess's smile symbolize in terms of reality versus illusion?

- How can this tale guide us in understanding the balance between love, obsession, and detachment?

The Dog's Vow in Winter, While Building Its House in Summer

In winter, when the weather grew cold, the dog's body shrank from the chill, and its whole being trembled from the cold. The biting cold bothered it so much that it thought to itself, "With this weak body I have, I need to build a stone house to protect myself from the freezing cold." So it decided, "This summer, I will build a stone house for myself so that next winter I won't suffer so much."

But when summer arrived and the cold no longer troubled it, the dog felt comfortable. Its bones loosened, and its skin stretched, making it look fatter and stronger. Seeing this, it thought, "With this strong body, where would I fit in such a small house?" It lay down in the shade, becoming lazy, full, weak, and stubborn—and it did nothing to prepare for the coming winter.

Its inner wisdom told it, "You have seen this winter, and another will come. So build a house so you won't suffer so much from the cold again." But the dog replied, "What house can hold this strong, fat body of mine?" and made no effort.

(Rumi, Masnavi-e Manavi)

Suggested Reflection and Exercise

1. Personal Reflection:

Think about a time when you promised yourself to change a habit or behavior after facing a difficult situation but then forgot about that promise when things got easier. What stopped you from following through? How did that affect you later?

2. Broader Perspective:

Why do you think people, like the dog, often delay preparing for future challenges when the present moment feels comfortable? How does this relate to human nature and our tendency to avoid discomfort?

3. Questions for Discussion or Writing:

- How can we stay motivated to keep our promises to ourselves, especially when immediate problems seem to go away?

- What practical steps can we take to plan ahead and build resilience even when times are good?

- Can you think of examples from history, society, or personal life where preparing early has helped avoid bigger problems later?

Suggested Practical Activity:

Future-Planning Journal: For one week, write down one small thing you can do each day to prepare for a future challenge or goal. Reflect at the end of the week how it feels to take these steps consistently.

Three Pieces of Advice

A man once caught a parrot, in the hopes of keeping him for company. The bird said to him, "I am of no use to you as a captive. But set me free, and I will tell you three valuable pieces of advice."

The bird promised to give the first piece of advice while still in the man's grasp, the second when he reached a branch, the third after he had reached the top of a mountain.

The man agreed, and asked for the first piece of advice.

The bird said, "If you lose something, even if it be valued by you as much as life itself—do not regret it."

Now the man let the bird go, and it hopped to a branch.

"Never believe anything that is contrary to sense, without proof." It continued.

Then the bird flew to the mountaintop. From here it squawked:

"Oh, how unfortunate for you! Within me are two huge jewels, and if you had only killed me, they would have been yours!"

The man was anguished at the thought of what he had lost.

"At least now tell me the third piece of advice."

The bird responded, "What an idiot you are, asking for more advice when you have not given thought to the first two pieces! I told you not to worry about what had been lost, and not to believe in something contrary to sense. Now you are doing both. You are believing something ridiculous and grieving because you have lost something! I am not big enough to have huge jewels inside me. You are a fool, sir! Stay down on the ground and think about these lessons I have imparted."

Awfi (1363).

Suggested Reflection and Exercise
1. Personal Reflection:
- Have you ever ignored good advice and later realized the consequences?

- Do you often regret missed opportunities or dwell on what might have been?

2. Broader Perspective:
- This story illustrates the gap between hearing wisdom and applying it.

- It challenges us to evaluate how often emotion overrides reason, even when we've been warned.

3. Questions for Discussion or Writing:

- Why is it easier to admire wisdom than to practice it?

- What does the story suggest about human nature and decision-making?

- In what situations do people tend to believe the unbelievable?

4. Suggested Practical Activity:

- Recall a recent situation where you made a quick emotional decision. Re-examine it using the bird's two initial pieces of advice. What would you do differently now?

Still Carrying Her

A pair of Buddhist monks came across a stream in their travels. It was running fast and underneath there was a bed of jagged rocks. The monks noticed a beautiful, young woman who couldn't swim. She called out to them, pleading with them to carry her across it. One was an old master of almost ninety and the other was a young novice only in his twenties.

The young woman said, "Masters, the stream is flooded. I can't swim. Will you help me across?"

The young monk was horrified at her request and replied, "No madam, I'm sorry, we're sworn to chastity and I can't carry you across the stream. I can't touch a woman. I can't do it."

The old monk thought for a moment and then said, "Alright I'll help you."

So, he took this beautiful young woman in his arms, had her put her lovely arms around his neck and her breasts close to his body and he carefully carried her across the stream. She thanked him very much, and they both went their separate ways.

Several hours passed, and still the young monk could not get over the old monk's unchaste behavior.

Finally, he said, "Master, how could you do a horrible thing like that? Take this beautiful young woman in your arms, let her put her lovely arms around your neck and her luscious breasts so close to you and carry her across the stream like that?"

And the old monk said, his face curled in a smirk, "My son, you're still carrying her."

Reps & Senzaki (1957).

Suggested Reflection and Exercise

1. Personal Reflection:

- Have you ever mentally held on to something long after the moment had passed?

- What effect did it have on your peace of mind or relationships?

2. Broader Perspective:

- The story highlights the difference between physical action and mental attachment.

- It questions the value of rigid rule-following when compassion is at stake.

- True discipline lies in letting go—not just of actions but of lingering thoughts.

3. Questions for Discussion or Writing:
- What does the young monk's reaction say about inner attachment versus outer restraint?

- How does the elder monk model wisdom beyond rules?

- In what ways do we all "carry" things unnecessarily?

4. Suggested Practical Activity:

- Take five minutes to reflect on something you're still holding on to—regret, resentment, worry. Write it down, then consciously decide to release it, either by tearing the paper or performing another symbolic act of letting go.

The Fox and the Grapes

On a hot summer's day a fox spied a bunch of succulent-looking grapes hanging high up from a vine. It was sweltering hot, and the fox could not pass up an opportunity for something to drink.

"These grapes are just what I need to quench my thirst!" exclaimed the fox.

But the vine on which the grapes hung was too high for him to reach even with his longest stretch. And so, he realized he would have to jump. Drawing back a few paces, he ran toward the vine and took a great leap upwards but fell just short of the grapes. Turning around, he jumped again. This time, too he failed. The fox tried to jump for the grapes again and again and again, to no avail.

Since he could not reach the delicious-looking grapes, the fox finally concluded, "These grapes must be sour."

And so he walked away with his nose in the air, hotter and thirstier than when he started.

Aesop (2006).

Suggested Reflection and Exercise

1. Personal Reflection:

- Can you recall a time when you gave up on something important by convincing yourself it wasn't worth it?

- How did that rationalization affect your feelings about the situation and yourself?

2. Broader Perspective:

- The story illustrates how we sometimes protect our self-esteem by devaluing what we cannot attain.

- This "sour grapes" mindset can prevent us from honestly facing challenges or seeking alternatives.

- Recognizing this bias can help us approach setbacks with more honesty and growth.

3. Questions for Discussion or Writing:

- Why do people sometimes tell themselves "the grapes are sour" instead of admitting a goal is difficult?

- How can this attitude hinder personal growth or problem-solving?

- What strategies can help us stay motivated even when we face repeated failure?

4. Suggested Practical Activity:

- Identify a goal you've recently given up on or rationalized as "not worth it."

- Reflect on your true feelings about it and write down alternative ways you might approach the challenge.

- Consider seeking advice or trying a small new step toward that goal before dismissing it completely.

Overcoming Fear of Rejection

Albert Ellis, the founder of Rational Emotive Behavior Therapy, recalls, "I was scared shitless of approaching women. I flirted with them in Bronx Botanical Garden near my home, but I never approached them, made up all kinds of excuses. So I gave myself a brilliant homework assignment at the age of 19 when I was off college, to go to Bronx Botanical Garden every day that month, and whenever I saw a woman sitting alone on a park bench, I would sit immediately next to her – not in her lap – which I hadn't dared do before, and give myself one lousy minute to talk to her. If I die, I die, screw it so I die. And I did that. I found 130 women sitting alone that month on the park bench. I sat next to all of them, whereupon 30 got up and walked away, but that left me an even sample of 100 good for research purposes. I spoke to the whole hundred for the first time in my life about the birds and the bees, the flowers, their reading.

And if Fred Skinner, who was then teaching at Indiana University, had known about my exploits, he would have thought I would have got extinguished, because of the hundred women I made one date and she didn't show up. But I prepared myself philosophically even then—it was before cognitive therapy really—by seeing that nobody took out a stiletto and cut my balls off, nobody vomited and ran away, nobody called the cops. I had a hundred pleasant conversations and in the second hundred I got good and made a few dates."

And Albert learned he wouldn't die from rejection and that it was not the end of the world. He even tried with a second 100 when he got good and even made a few dates, and as he said, "got to be one of the best picker-uppers of women in the United States."

Ellis, A. (2004).

Suggested Reflection and Exercise

1. Personal Reflection:

- Think about a fear or challenge that has held you back. How have you avoided facing it?

- How might facing small steps, like Ellis did, change your experience and confidence?

2. Broader Perspective:

- Ellis's story highlights the power of exposure and persistence in overcoming fears.

- It shows how re-framing failure (rejection) as a learning experience reduces anxiety and builds resilience.

- This approach can apply to many areas, not just social fears.

3. Questions for Discussion or Writing:

- What fears or anxieties do you avoid confronting, and why?

- How can breaking down a big fear into manageable, repeatable actions help overcome it?

- How does changing your interpretation of failure affect your motivation?

4. Suggested Practical Activity:

- Identify one small, manageable action you can take toward facing a personal fear or challenge.

- Set a goal to repeat this action regularly for a week or a month.

- Keep a journal to note your feelings before, during, and after each attempt, focusing on what you learn rather than the outcome.

The Power of our View

Two thousand years ago, Epictetus was a Greek slave to Roman masters. He demonstrated how he could not be upset when terrible things happened to him. He was a slave, and he had chains on his legs, and the master who owned him started tightening the chain on his leg, and he said calmly, "Master, if you keep tightening those chains you'll break my leg."

The master did break his leg and he would be a cripple for the rest of his life.

Epictetus said to the master who had crippled him, his voice flat and equable,

"See, you broke my leg."

The master was so impressed he freed him, and Epictetus went on to be a philosophical leader in Rome, all through his own reasoning.

Albert Ellis, the founder of Rational Emotive Behavior Therapy (REBT) then spoke of one of the cornerstones of REBT, paraphrasing Epictetus, "It's not the bad things that happen that upset you, it's your view of them."

Epictetus (2008).

Suggested Reflection and Exercise
1. Personal Reflection:
- Recall a situation where your reaction caused you more distress than the event itself. How might changing your interpretation have changed your feelings?

- How do you currently handle events that feel out of your control?

2. Broader Perspective:
- Epictetus teaches that while we cannot always control what happens, we can control how we interpret and respond to it.

- This idea forms the basis for cognitive therapies like REBT, emphasizing the power of mindset in emotional well-being.

- It invites us to take responsibility for our own emotional states rather than blaming external circumstances.

3. Questions for Discussion or Writing:

- What does it mean to "own" your emotional responses?

- How can changing your perspective on a challenging event reduce emotional pain?

- Can you identify any beliefs you hold that might be causing unnecessary upset?

4. Suggested Practical Activity:
- Next time you feel upset, pause and write down the event and your initial emotional reaction.

- Then, try to reframe the situation from a different, more neutral or positive viewpoint.

- Reflect on how this shift changes your feelings. Practice this regularly to build emotional resilience.

Three Ways to Tolerance

Albert Ellis, the founder of Rational Emotive Behavior Therapy (REBT), always talked about three ways of tolerance as the roads to happiness and psychological well-being. When he was asked what the three ways were. He said:

Unconditional self-acceptance means that you do not tolerate your destructive demands—your absolutistic shoulds, oughts, and musts—but replace them with flexible preferences, "I would distinctly like to do well and win the approval of others, but I don't have to do so. If and when I fail and get rejected, I can always accept myself, my being, while remaining intolerant of some of my behaviors."

Unconditional other-acceptance means that you do not tolerate the antisocial and sabotaging actions of other people, and you try to help them change. But you always accept them, their personhood, and you never damn their total selves. You tolerate their humanity while disagreeing with some of their actions.

Unconditional life-acceptance means that you deplore adversities and injustices and do your best to rectify them. But when you can't change inevitable misfortunes, you un-upsettably accept them and do not get enraged, panic, or depress yourself about them.

(The Albert Ellis website: https://www.rebtnetwork.org).

Suggested Reflection and Exercise
1. Personal Reflection:
- Reflect on your own "shoulds" and "musts." How rigid or flexible are your expectations for yourself, others, and life?

- Think of a recent situation where you struggled to accept yourself, another person, or a difficult life event. How might unconditional acceptance have changed your experience?

2. Broader Perspective:
- These three types of tolerance balance compassion with boundaries: accepting the person while rejecting harmful behavior.

- They encourage emotional resilience by separating identity from actions and outcomes.

- Practicing this can reduce unnecessary suffering and improve relationships and well-being.

3. Questions for Discussion or Writing:
- How do you differentiate between accepting someone and tolerating harmful behavior?

- What challenges do you face when trying to accept life's inevitable hardships?

- Can unconditional self-acceptance lead to complacency, or does it empower growth? Why?

4. Suggested Practical Activity:
- Choose one area—self, others, or life—where you struggle with acceptance. Write down your typical "should" or demand.

- Reframe it as a flexible preference (e.g., "I would like to... but I don't have to…").

The Wayward Princess

A certain king believed unquestioningly in the lessons he had been taught and the beliefs he had been ingrained with by his forefathers. He was a just man in his own right, but could not see beyond the confines of what he had been taught.

One day he was lecturing his three daughters:

"All that I have will someday be yours. Through me you obtained your life. It is my will which determines your future, and hence determines your fate."

Respectfully and quite persuaded of the truth of this, two of the girls agreed.

The third daughter, however, countered, "Although my position demands that I be obedient to the laws, I cannot believe that my fate must always be determined by you."

"We shall see about that," said the king.

He ordered her to be imprisoned in a dark cell in the furthest corner of his dungeon, where she lost track of time in the perpetual darkness. Meanwhile, the king and his obedient daughters spent their wealth without a care in the world that would otherwise have been spent upon her.

The king mused to himself; "This girl lies in prison not by her own will, but by mine. This proves, sufficiently for any logical mind, that it is my will, not hers, which determines her fate."

The people of the country, hearing of their princess's situation, said to one another:

"She must have done or said something terrible to the king, with whom we find no fault, to treat his own flesh and blood in such a way." For they had not arrived at the point where they felt the need to dispute the king's assumption of being right in everything.

From time to time the king would visit his daughter. Although she was pale and weakened from her imprisonment, she refused to change her attitude. Finally, the king's patience came to an end.

"Your continued disobedience," he said to her, "will only annoy me further, and it may be seen to weaken my rights if you stay within my realms. I could kill you, but as I am merciful I will banish you into the wilderness next to my lands. This is a wilderness, inhabited only by wild beasts and outcasts who cannot survive in our rational society. There you will soon discover whether you can have an existence apart from that of your family; and, if you can, whether you prefer it to ours."

His announcement was at once obeyed, and she was taken to the borders of the kingdom. The princess found herself set loose in a wild land that bore little resemblance to the sheltered surroundings of her upbringing. But she quickly learned that a cave would serve as a house, that nuts and fruit came from trees and that warmth came from the sun. This wilderness had a climate and a way of existing of its own.

After some time she had so ordered her life that she had water from springs, vegetables from the earth and even fire from a smoldering tree.

"Here," she said to herself, "is a life whose elements belong together;

they form a completeness. Yet neither individually nor collectively do they obey the commands of my father the king."

One day a lost traveler—as it happened a man of great riches —came upon the exiled princess, fell in love with her, and took her back to his own country, where they were married. After a space of time, the two decided to return to the wilderness where they built a huge and prosperous city where their wisdom, resources and faith were expressed to their fullest possible extent. The oddities and outcasts, many of them thought to be madmen, all took up a role within this framework and each came to know a singular contentedness with their place in this city.

The city and its surrounding countryside became renowned throughout the entire world. It was not long before its power and beauty eclipsed that of the realm of the princess's father.

By the common choice of the population, the princess and her husband were elected to the joint monarchy of this new kingdom.

The King decided to visit the strange and mysterious place which had sprung up from nothing in the wilderness and which was, he heard, populated at least in part by those whom he and his people despised. As he slowly approached the foot of the throne upon which the young couple sat and raised his eyes to meet those whose names for justice, prosperity and understanding far exceeded his own, he was able to catch the murmured words of his daughter:

"You see, Father, every man and woman has his or her own fate and choice."

Idries Shah (1971).

Suggested Reflection and Exercise

1. Personal Reflection:

Think about a time when you faced opposition or limitations imposed by others, especially those close to you. How did you respond? Did you find your own path despite the obstacles, or did you conform? Reflect on what this story teaches about personal agency and fate.

2. Broader Perspective:

Consider the societal structures or traditions that limit individual freedom. How does the story challenge the idea that one's future is solely determined by inherited authority or family? What does it suggest about creating new communities based on shared values and acceptance?

3. Questions for Discussion or Writing:

- What does the princess's journey say about the balance between obedience and independence?

- How does exile lead to growth and transformation in the story?

- What role does choice play in shaping destiny?

- Why do you think the people eventually accept the princess's new kingdom?

The Son Who Killed his Mother

A man, filled with anger and suspicion, killed his mother with both a dagger and his fists. When he was asked why he did such a terrible thing, someone said, "How could you forget the respect owed to a mother? Tell me, why did you kill her? What wrong did she do?"

He replied, "She committed a disgraceful act, so shameful that only the earth should cover it. I killed her to bury her shame with her."

The other person asked, "Then why didn't you kill the man who was involved with her?"

The man answered, "If I did, I'd have to kill a man every day. By killing her, I saved myself from shedding the blood of many. It's better to end her life than to kill countless others."

That wicked mother, whose faults spread far and wide, is like the sinful part of your own soul. You must destroy it, because of it, you are constantly fighting—with God and with people. The world feels narrow and harsh because of this inner conflict.

If you have killed this sinful part within you, you no longer need to defend yourself—no one in the world will be your enemy.

(Rumi, Masnavi-e Manavi).

Suggested Reflection and Exercise

1. Personal Reflection:

- Reflect on a part of yourself (e.g., pride, anger, envy, resentment) that repeatedly causes conflict in your life.

- Have you ever blamed others for something rooted in your own unresolved inner struggle?

- What would it mean to "end" or transform that destructive part of yourself?

2. Broader Perspective:

- This story is symbolic. The "mother" represents the source of internal corruption. Consider how destructive behaviors often stem from within rather than from outside forces.

- In many spiritual and psychological traditions, transformation comes not from controlling others but from self-purification.

- What might the story be saying about the nature of real enemies—are they external or internal?

3. Questions for Discussion or Writing:

- What does "killing the sinful part of your soul" mean to you?

- How does inner conflict affect your view of the world and your relationships?

- Can the act of confronting your own darkness bring peace? Why or why not?

Suggested Practical Activity:
- Shadow Awareness Journal:

For one week, journal moments when you feel blame, anger, jealousy, or judgment. Try to trace each reaction inward—what part of you is being triggered? What belief or insecurity lies beneath it? At the end of the week, write a reflection on what part of your "inner self" needs healing or letting go.

The Toothless Cobra

Indian folklore tells of a Swami who lived within a temple. He was troubled by the lack of visitors. It turned out they were fearful of a cobra living on the road leading there. The Swami decided to try and persuade the snake not to attack passers-by, as those people were surely pious and devoted to their religion, given their journeying all this way. The snake agreed and over time the temple started to fill with visitors. Pleased with the result, the Swami made his way to the snake to thank him. However, he found the snake in poor condition; his body was riddled with cuts and scrapes, and a look of utter dejection hung on the creature's face. The snake explained that, since he had stopped biting, people had lost their fear of the snake. Even small children would come and pelt the snake with rocks while he cowered. The Swami was shocked to hear this. He soon realized the error of the snake's ways: he had asked the snake to stop biting, but he had never stopped him from hissing.

De Vos, G. (2003).

Suggested Reflection and Exercise

1. Personal Reflection:

Think about a time when you gave up a part of yourself to please others or to avoid conflict, but it caused unexpected difficulties. How did it affect your sense of identity or well-being?

2. Broader Perspective:

Consider the importance of boundaries and self-expression in relationships and communities. How can losing an essential part of oneself, even for a good cause, lead to vulnerability or misunderstanding?

3. Questions for Discussion or Writing:
- What might the cobra's biting and hissing represent in terms of personal boundaries or self-defense?

- Why is it important to maintain some form of "warning" or assertiveness even when we want peace?

- How can we balance being approachable and kind without becoming an easy target for harm?

4. Suggested Practical Activity:

Reflect on your own ways of setting boundaries—verbally or non-verbally. Practice expressing your limits clearly in a small situation where you tend to give in. Afterwards, note how this affected your comfort and the response of others.

Overcoming our Past Actions

A cow and her calf underwent daily torment at the hand of their Brahmin owner. The cow decided that, for the sake of herself and her calf, she would gore the owner to death. However, the calf cautioned her mother against such action.

"We are presently suffering for the consequences of our past actions. If we murder our owner now, all we are doing is perpetuating a cycle of violent actions and consequences. We can overcome the consequences of our past actions only when we undergo them with composure, courage and dignity."

Rennie, D. (1994).

Suggested Reflection and Exercise
1. Personal Reflection:
Reflect on a situation where you felt wronged or hurt by someone's actions. How did your reaction either continue a cycle of negativity or help break it? What feelings did you experience when you chose patience or restraint?

2. Broader Perspective:
Consider the idea of karma or consequences in life. How does responding to hardship with composure and dignity affect not only yourself but those around you? Can forgiveness or patience change the course of difficult cycles?

3. Questions for Discussion or Writing:
- What does it mean to "overcome" the consequences of past actions rather than react to them?

- How can courage and dignity help in breaking cycles of violence or harm?

- Are there times when action is necessary, and how do we decide the right moment?

4. Suggested Practical Activity:

Identify a current challenge or conflict in your life. Practice responding to it with calmness and thoughtful restraint for a set period (a day, a week). Journal how this approach changes your feelings and the situation's development.

Terrible Tempers

A monk once asked of his master, "I have a terrible, uncontrollable temper and I cannot deal with it any longer. Please help me."

"Well, show it to me and I will see what I can do." said the master.

"I am sorry, at the moment I don't have it."

"Well, the next time you have it, bring it before me!"

The monk hesitated.

"I am not sure I can do that." admitted the monk.

"In that case it is not yours," declared the master, "and if it returns, I suggest you get hold of it and then beat it away with a stick!"

Otto, M. (2000).

Suggested Reflection and Exercise

1. Personal Reflection:

Think about a time when you felt overwhelmed by anger or frustration. How did you handle it? Could stepping back and observing your temper as something separate from yourself help you manage it better?

2. Broader Perspective:

How do different cultures or philosophies understand anger and emotions? Consider the idea that emotions like anger may not truly belong to us but are temporary states that can be controlled.

3. Questions for Discussion or Writing:

- What does the master mean by "if it returns, get hold of it and then beat it away"?

- Can anger be seen as a visitor rather than a permanent resident? How might this change how we relate to it?

- How can awareness and timing help us respond to emotions effectively?

4. Suggested Practical Activity:

The next time you feel anger rising, pause and try to observe it without acting on it immediately. Note where you feel it in your body and what thoughts arise. Practice "holding" your temper gently and then consciously choosing a calm response.

Don't Think of Monkeys

Milarepa was a monk renowned throughout Tibet for his foresight and perceptiveness. A gentleman who felt very agitated came to Milarepa seeking advice. He claimed that an ever-present ringing noise in his head had made him restless and irritable for many weeks. He asked Milarepa for a way of stopping this clamor that occupied his mind. Milarepa told him to go home and to stop thinking of monkeys. The gentleman said that thinking of monkeys was not a problem for him, because monkeys did not cross his mind. Milarepa was delighted to hear this and declared that, in that case, the practice of not thinking about monkeys should then come very easily to him. He told the man to go home and continue to practice. The gentleman began to do what he was told, only to realize that the harder he tried not to think of monkeys, the more he ended up thinking of monkeys. Meanwhile, the ringing noise had disappeared.

Pernicano, P. (2015).

Suggested Reflection and Exercise
1. Personal Reflection:
Reflect on a time when trying not to think about something only made you think about it more. How did that affect your feelings or stress? What does this say about the way our minds work?

2. Broader Perspective:
Consider how attempts to suppress certain thoughts can often backfire. How do mindfulness and acceptance-based approaches differ from trying to force thoughts away?

3. Questions for Discussion or Writing:
- Why do you think Milarepa told the gentleman to stop thinking about monkeys, even though monkeys weren't on his mind initially?

- How can this story illustrate the paradox of thought suppression?

- What might be a more effective way to handle unwanted or intrusive thoughts?

4. Suggested Practical Activity:

Next time an unwanted thought or noise bothers you, try simply noticing it without trying to push it away. Observe how it changes or fades when you stop fighting it. Write about your experience afterward.

The Three Fish

There was a shallow pond of water where three fish lived. One was very clever, one was of average intelligence and the other was very stupid. Life continued monotonously for the fish, day in, day out until one day a human arrived, carrying a net with him. The first fish, calling upon his intellect and experience, decided to take action. The pool was devoid of shelter—there were few places to hide. Thus, the fish decided his best option would be to play dead. He summoned all his strength and leapt from the water onto the land, holding his breath as he did. He lay at the fisherman's feet, but the man supposed the animal was dead and simply threw him back into the pond. Now, the second fish, which was not as clever, inquired about what he was doing.

"Simple," responded the gifted fish, "I merely pretended to be dead, so he tossed me back in the water."

Heeding this advice, the second fish jumped out of the water right at the fisherman.

"Such a strange thing," mused the man, "they are jumping up and about all over the place."

Unfortunately for the second fish, he forgot to hold his breath, so the fisherman knew him to be alive and added him to his catch. The fisherman looked back into the pond, taken aback by the peculiar actions of the fish and he forgot to close his satchel. The second fish, upon noticing this, managed to wriggle himself out of the satchel and rolled right back into the pond. Exhausted from almost suffocating, the second fish made his way to the intelligent fish and lay beside him.

The idiot fish had watched both his counterparts, but made nothing of their capture and escape. He continued to stare blankly at the pair. So, to save their friend, the two other fish went over every point with him, slowly and methodically, so that he might avoid falling prey to the man.

"Thank you so much! I now know what I must do." said the stupid fish.

With that he jumped from the water and landed right beside the fisherman, holding his breath. The fisherman, exasperated, simply grabbed the fish without checking if it was alive or dead. He tossed it in the satchel, this time making sure he closed it. Then he swept the pond with his net, but found nothing. The other two fish had managed to hide themselves in a depression under the bank. He gave up, looked at the unmoving fish in his bag, and then promptly took it home and fed it to his cat.

(Rumi, Masnavi-e Manavi).

Suggested Reflection and Exercise

1. Personal Reflection:

Think about a situation where you had to act quickly or cleverly to avoid a problem or danger. How did your own intelligence or intuition help you? Were there times when acting without thinking caused trouble?

2. Broader Perspective:

Consider how knowledge and experience can increase our chances of survival or success, but also how luck and circumstances affect outcomes. How do different approaches to problem-solving shape the results in life?

3. Questions for Discussion or Writing:

- What does the story say about intelligence and its role in survival?

- How does the story portray the "stupid" fish's fate? Could the outcome have been different?

- What lessons can be drawn about teaching and learning from others' experiences?

4. Suggested Practical Activity:

Reflect on a recent challenge you faced. Write down how you approached it and whether you used lessons from past experiences or others' advice. Then consider how you might improve your responses in the future by observing and learning more carefully.

Being on Top

There was a merchant who had been a respected and prominent member of his community for many years. Despite his status, he was fearful that his daughter might bring shame on his family. For before his very eyes, she had transformed from a little girl into an enchanting young woman who attracted the gaze of many men.

He warned her, "My daughter, sinful and devious are the ways of these young men. You must be cautious when you deal with them, so that you do not bring disgrace on yourself and on your family."

Now that he had his daughter's attention, he continued, "Men are after one thing. They are single-minded in their lustful desires. My only wish is to protect you from harm and embarrassment. So, listen carefully to what I say so that you know how to protect yourself when the time comes. First, the man will admire you, praising your beauty and your charms. Then he will flatter you and invite you to spend time with him. Soon he will walk you by his house, as if by chance, and remember that there is something of vital importance he must get from inside. Of course, he will invite you inside whilst he looks for it. While waiting, he will offer you a seat and a drink out of politeness. He will sit beside you and the two of you will listen to music together. Then finally, when the moment is right, he will force himself on top of you and you will be violated—your family shamed and your reputation ruined."

The daughter was greatly impressed by her father's speech in all its passion and energy. She promised her father that she would take heed of every word and swore to protect herself and the family name.

Some time later she approached her father in reverence, "Are you a magician?" She inquired.

"It was exactly as you predicted. First me admired me, and then invited me out. After that, the dear boy took me to his house and invited me inside. Once I was inside, he offered me a drink, just as you predicted. Before long, we were listening to soft and soothing music. All this time I was remembering your words and I knew exactly what was about to happen. Just when he was about to make his move, I forced myself on top of him instead; I violated him and shamed him and his family!"

(Rumi, Masnavi-e Manavi).

Suggested Reflection and Exercise

1. Personal Reflection:

Think about a time when you were given advice that seemed strict or cautionary but later realized its deeper wisdom. How did you react initially, and how did your understanding evolve? How does this story challenge or reinforce your ideas about control, power, and agency in difficult situations?

2. Broader Perspective:

Consider how societal expectations, gender roles, or cultural norms influence behavior in relationships and power dynamics. How might this story reflect or critique those norms? What can it teach us about taking control of one's narrative rather than being a passive participant?

3. Questions for Discussion or Writing:

- How does the daughter's response flip the usual narrative about vulnerability and power?

- What lessons about foresight, preparedness, and courage does the story convey?

- Can this story apply beyond romantic or gendered contexts? How?

Socrates and the Triple Filter Test

One day, a man came running to Socrates, eager to share some gossip. He said, "Socrates, I have to tell you something about your friend!"

Socrates calmly raised his hand and replied, "Wait. Before you tell me anything, let's put it through the Triple Filter Test." "Triple filter?" the man asked.

"Yes," Socrates said. "Before you talk to me about someone else, let's filter what you're going to say.

First filter—Truth:

Are you absolutely sure that what you're about to say is true?"

The man replied, "Well… no, I just heard it…"

Socrates nodded, "So you don't really know if it's true or not."

Second filter—Goodness:

"Is what you're about to say something good?"

"No… actually, it's quite the opposite…"

Socrates continued, "So you want to tell me something bad about someone, and you're not sure if it's even true?"

Third filter – Usefulness:

"Is what you're going to say useful to me?"

The man hesitated, "Not really…"

"Then," Socrates said, "If what you want to say is not true, not good, and not useful, why say it at all?"

(Anonymous).

Suggested Reflection and Exercise

1. Personal Reflection:

Think of a recent time when you were about to share or hear gossip or judgmental talk. Did you pause to consider if the information was true, kind, or useful? How did your choice—either to speak or stay silent—affect you or others involved?

2. Broader Perspective:

In today's world of constant information sharing—especially on social media—Socrates' wisdom remains relevant. Speaking without reflection can harm relationships, reputations, and even social harmony. Using thoughtful filters helps create a more respectful and trustworthy environment.

3. Questions for Discussion or Writing:

- Why do you think people often feel compelled to share unverified or negative information?

- How might your relationships improve if you practiced the Triple Filter Test regularly?

- Can silence sometimes be more powerful than speaking?

4. Suggested Practical Activity:
Filter Practice Journal:

For one week, keep a brief journal of moments when you either chose to share or withhold information. Each time, ask yourself: Was it true? Was it good? Was it useful? Reflect on how this practice impacted your interactions.

Love is Best

One morning, a woman walked out of her front door, only to see three elderly, bearded gentlemen sitting in her yard. She had no clue who any of these men were.

She walked up to them and said, "I don't think I know you, but you look famished. If you like, please come in and have something to eat."

"Is the man of the house home?" one of the men asked.

"No," she answered, "he's out."

"Then I'm afraid we cannot come in."

In the evening when her husband came home, she told him what had happened.

"Well, now that I'm home, you'd best go out and invite them in!" her husband said.

The woman went out and invited the men in once more.

"We do not go into a house together," they replied.

"Why is that?"

"Well," began one of the old men, "we are here to help you. His name is Wealth."

He pointed to the man beside him.

"He is Success." he continued, pointing to the third man.

"And I am Love."

Then he added, "Now go back in and discuss with your husband which one of us you want to invite into your life."

The woman went in and told her husband what was said. Her husband was overjoyed.

"How wonderful! I think we should invite in Wealth. Let him come and fill our home with wealth!"

His wife disagreed, "My dear, why don't we invite Success?"

Their daughter was listening from the other corner of the house. She jumped in with her own suggestion:

"Wouldn't it be better to invite Love into our home? Our life will then be filled with love!"

"Let us heed our daughter's advice," said the husband to his wife.

"Go out and invite Love to be our guest."

The woman went out and asked the three old men, "Which one of you is Love? Please come in and be our guest."

Love rose to his feet and started walking toward the house. The other two also got up and followed right behind him.

Surprised, the lady asked Wealth and Success, "I only invited Love;

why are you coming also?" The old men replied together, "If you had invited Wealth or Success, the other two of us would've stayed out, but since you invited Love, wherever he goes, we go with him. Wherever there is Love, Wealth and Success will always follow."

(Author unknown, n.d.). Love, Wealth, and Success. Retrieved from https://www.skywriting.net/inspirational/stories/the_invitation.htm.

Suggested Reflection and Exercise

1. Personal Reflection:

Think about times when you prioritized material success, wealth, or status over love or relationships. How did those choices affect your happiness and well-being? Have you experienced moments when choosing love first led to better outcomes in your life? Reflect on how your own priorities shape your daily decisions.

2. Broader Perspective:

Consider how society often values wealth and success over kindness, compassion, and love. What are some examples where this value system influences communities, workplaces, or families? How might the story's message challenge or inspire changes in how society defines true success?

3. Questions for Discussion or Writing:

- Why do you think Love attracts Wealth and Success, but not necessarily the other way around?

- How can inviting "Love" into your life impact your relationships and goals?

- Can you think of a situation where focusing on love or kindness changed the outcome positively?

- How might this story relate to the earlier "Two Wolves" story about the choices we make inside ourselves?

4. Suggested Practical Activity:

For one week, practice consciously "inviting Love" into your daily interactions. This could mean showing extra kindness, listening deeply, expressing gratitude, or offering support without expecting anything in return. Keep a journal of any changes you notice in your mood, relationships, or opportunities. Reflect on whether Love truly seems to bring "Wealth and Success" into your life.

Two Wolves

An old Cherokee man sat with his grandson. He hoped to teach the boy what his many years on this Earth had taught him about life.

"There is a fight going on inside me as we speak," he told the boy.

"It is a gruesome and interminable fight between two wolves. One is evil—he is anger, envy, sorrow, regret, greed, arrogance, self-pity, guilt, resentment, inferiority, lies, false pride and superiority. The other is good—he is joy, peace, love, hope, serenity, humility, kindness, benevolence, empathy, generosity, truth, compassion and faith. The same fight is going on inside you, and inside every other person, too."

The grandson thought about this for a minute; he then asked his grandfather, "Which wolf will win?"

The old Cherokee simply replied, "The one you feed."

Author unknown. (n.d.). Two Wolves (Cherokee legend). Retrieved from https://www.cherokee-legends.com/cherokee-indian-guide/164-native-american-legends-two-wolves-a-cherokee-legend.html.

Suggested Reflection and Exercise

1. Personal Reflection:

Think about the "two wolves" inside you—the positive and negative emotions or traits described in the story. Which wolf do you find yourself feeding most often? Are there specific situations or triggers that make you feed one wolf more than the other? Reflect on how your choices affect your mood, actions, and relationships.

2. Broader Perspective:

Consider how this inner fight is a universal human experience. How might recognizing this struggle in others increase your empathy or patience? How can communities or workplaces support people in "feeding the good wolf"?

3. Questions for Discussion or Writing:

- What practical steps can you take to "feed the good wolf" in your daily life?

- How do negative emotions like anger or envy impact your well-being and decision-making?

- Can you think of a time when feeding the good wolf changed a difficult situation for the better?

- How does this story relate to the idea of personal responsibility for your thoughts and actions?

4. Suggested Practical Activity:

For the next few days, keep a simple log of moments when you notice yourself feeling or acting with either "good wolf" or "bad wolf" qualities. After each entry, write down one small action you can take to feed the good wolf next time. Review your log at the end of the week and reflect on any patterns or changes you notice.

The Most Important Part

When I was small, my mother would ask me what the most important part of the body is. Through the years I would take a guess at what I thought might be the correct answer. When I was first asked, I thought sound and hearing what others have to say were very important to us as people.

So, I told her, "My ears, mummy."

She said, "No. Many people are deaf, but they still live complete lives. But you keep thinking about it, I will ask you again soon."

Several years passed before she asked me this question again. Since making my first attempt, I had spent many afternoons contemplating the right answer.

This time, I told her, "Mummy, sight is very important to everybody, so it must be our eyes." she looked at me and told me, smiling, "You are learning fast, but the answer is not correct because there are many people around us who are blind."

Stumped once more, I continued my search for possible answers. Over the years, Mother asked me several more times.

Always, her answer was, "No, but you are getting smarter every year, my child."

Then, last year, my grandfather died suddenly and unexpectedly. Everybody was hurt. Everybody was crying. Even my father, who I had never seen shed a tear, wept for days. My mum looked me straight in the eyes when it was our turn to say our final goodbye to grandpa. She took my hand and asked me, "Do you know the most important body part yet, my dear?"

I was shocked when she asked me this now. I always thought this was a game between her and me. She saw the confusion on my face and told me.

"This question is very important. It shows the way that you have really lived your life. For every body part you gave me in the past, I have told you that you were wrong and I have given you an example of why. But today is the day you need to learn this important lesson."

She looked down at me in the way only a mother can. I saw her eyes begin to well up with tears.

She said, "My dear, the most important body part is your shoulder."

I asked, "Is it because it holds up your head?"

"No," she replied, "it is because it can hold the head of a friend or loved one when they cry. Everybody will need a shoulder to cry on sometime in their life, my dear. I only hope that you have enough love and friends that you will have a shoulder to cry on when you need it someday."

Then and there I knew the most important body part was not a selfish one. It is that which is sympathetic to the pain of others.

Author unknown. (n.d.). The Most Important Part. Retrieved from https://www.motivateus.com.

Suggested Reflection and Exercise

1. Personal Reflection:

Think about a time when you have needed a "shoulder to cry on" or when you have offered one to someone else. How did that experience affect you? How do you view the role of empathy and support in your relationships?

2. Broader Perspective:

Consider the idea that the most important part of ourselves is not physical, but emotional and relational. How does this perspective challenge common values in today's fast-paced, achievement-focused society? What might change if more people valued emotional support as highly as physical health or success?

3. Questions for Discussion or Writing:

- Why do you think the mother repeatedly said the child's answers were wrong before revealing the truth?

- How does the story redefine strength and importance in human connection?

- What does it mean to "have enough love and friends to have a shoulder to cry on?" How can we cultivate that in our lives?

The Ant and the Grasshopper: Minimizing Risk

In a sunny meadow, there lived an ant and a grasshopper. During the warm summer months, the ant worked tirelessly, gathering tiny bits of food and storing them in her underground home. She scurried back and forth, carrying grains and seeds, always preparing for the winter ahead. The grasshopper, however, spent his days singing and dancing under the sun, hopping from blade to blade, enjoying the warmth without a care. He laughed at the ant's hard work, saying, "Why toil so much, friend? Come, sing with me and enjoy the summer!"

The ant replied, "I'm preparing for winter when food will be scarce. You should do the same." But the grasshopper waved her off, saying, "Winter is far away, and there's plenty of food now!"

As summer turned to autumn and then to winter, the meadow grew cold, and food vanished. The grasshopper, hungry and shivering, had nothing to eat. He went to the ant's home, where she was safe and well-fed from her stores. "Please, share some of your food," he begged. The ant, though kind, said, "I worked hard to prepare for this season while you sang. I have only enough for my family. Had you planned ahead, you wouldn't be hungry now."

The grasshopper limped away, learning too late the value of preparing to minimize the risk of hardship.

Townsend, G. F. (1867).

Suggested Reflection and Exercise

1. Personal Reflection:

- Think of a time when you chose short-term enjoyment over long-term preparation. What were the results?

- Do you tend to be more like the ant (planner) or the grasshopper (improviser) in your daily life? Why?

2. Broader Perspective:

- In what areas of modern life—such as health, finances, education, or relationships—do you think people often fail to prepare?

- How might preparation reduce the impact of unexpected challenges in those areas?

3. Questions for Discussion or Writing:

- Is it possible to find a balance between enjoying the present and preparing for the future?

- Should the ant have shared her food? Why or why not?

- What does this story suggest about personal responsibility and community support?

4. Suggested Practical Activity:

- Choose one aspect of your life (e.g., savings, learning, health) and make a one-week "ant plan":

- Write 2–3 small daily actions you can take to reduce future risk.

- At the end of the week, reflect on how it felt to act with preparation in mind.

The Pain of Pleasing Others

An old man, a boy and their donkey were going to town. The boy rode on the donkey while the old man walked beside him. As they went along, they passed some people who remarked what a shame; it was the old man was walking while the fit, young boy got to ride. The man and boy thought maybe the critics were right, so they changed positions.

A few minutes later, they passed some people who remarked, "What a shame, he makes that little boy walk."

So, they then decided they'd both walk. Soon they passed some more people who laughed at them, pointing out how stupid it was to walk when they had a decent donkey to ride right beside them. So, they decided to both ride the donkey. Now they passed some people who shamed them, saying how awful it was to put such a load on a poor donkey. The boy and man figured they were probably right, so they decided to carry the donkey. As they crossed a rickety bridge, they lost their grip on the animal and it fell into the river and drowned.

You might be wondering, "what is the moral of this story?" Well, if you try to please everyone, you might as well kiss your ass goodbye!

Salahi (2002).

Suggested Reflection and Exercise

1. Personal Reflection:

Think about a time when you tried to please everyone around you. How did it affect your decisions, feelings, or outcomes? Did you lose sight of what was truly important to you?

2. Broader Perspective:

This story shows how trying to satisfy everyone's opinions can lead to confusion, frustration, and even harm. It reminds us that it's impossible to please all people at all times and that we must trust our own judgment and values.

3. Questions for Discussion or Writing:

- Why do people feel pressured to please everyone?

- How can trying to please others negatively impact our lives?

- What strategies can help us balance others' opinions with our own needs?

4. Suggested Practical Activity:

Identify a situation where you felt pressured by others' opinions. Write down what you wanted to do versus what others expected. Reflect on how you can set boundaries and make decisions aligned with your values while still respecting others.

Unconditional Support as a Proactive Behavior

A boy was born to a couple after eleven years of marriage. They were a loving couple and the boy was the apple of their eye. One morning the husband saw a medicine bottle open. He was late for work so he asked his wife to cap the bottle and keep it in the cupboard, he was worried about their two-year-old son playing with it. His wife, preoccupied in the kitchen, completely forgot. The boy looked at the bottle in fascination, with all its vibrant colors. When his mum wasn't watching, he swallowed all its contents. When the child collapsed, the mother hurried him to the hospital, where he died, only hours later. The mother was beside herself with grief. She was terrified as to how she would face her husband. When the distraught father came to the hospital and saw his child lying before him, he looked at his wife and uttered just five words.

I am sure at this point you are wondering what a father could possibly say at a time such as this. Perhaps you are wondering, if you and him had traded places for just a moment, which words you would have uttered when you stepped into that room.

The husband simply gripped his wife and told her, "I am with you, darling."

This is what we might call proactive behavior. The child is dead, no angry outburst or accusation would ever change this. Finding fault with his wife, a mother who has lost her only child, would solve nothing. What she needed at that moment, more than anything else, was consolation and sympathy from the husband. This is what he gave her. If everyone lived like this, considering the outcomes of our words instead of being quick to say whatever made us feel better, then it would be a very different world indeed. Sometimes we all spend time asking who is responsible or who is to blame, whether in a relationship, in a job or with the people we know. When doing this we often end up doing irreparable damage to these relationships.

Fun with Stories (Uncle Teng).

Suggested Reflection and Exercise

1. Personal Reflection:

Recall a moment when someone offered you support without judgment during a difficult time. How did it affect your feelings and the relationship? Have you been able to provide such support to others?

2. Broader Perspective:

This story highlights the power of empathy and unconditional support in times of grief or crisis. Instead of blame or anger, offering compassion can help heal wounds and strengthen bonds, even in the face of tragedy.

3. Questions for Discussion or Writing:

- Why is it often difficult to withhold blame when things go wrong?

- How can unconditional support change the outcome of a painful situation?

- In what ways can we practice empathy proactively in our relationships?

4. Suggested Practical Activity:

Think of someone in your life who may be struggling. Reach out with a simple message of support or a listening ear, without offering advice or judgment. Reflect afterward on how this affected your connection and your own feelings.

Nails in the Fence

There once was a young boy who had a terrible temper. One day he flew into a particularly bad rage and his father gave him a bag of nails. He told his son that every time he lost his temper, he must hammer a nail into the back of the fence. By the end of the first day the boy had already driven 37 nails into the fence.

Over the next few weeks, as he learned to control his anger, the number of nails that he hammered each day gradually dwindled down. He discovered it was easier to hold his temper than to drive those nails into the fence. Finally, the day came when the boy didn't lose his temper once for the whole day. He excitedly told his father about his achievement. The father suggested that the boy now pull out one nail for each day that he was able to hold his temper.

The weeks passed and the young boy was finally able to tell his father that all the nails were gone. The father took his son by the hand and led him to the fence.

"You have done well, my son, but look at the holes in the fence. The fence will never be the same. When you say things in anger, they leave scars just like you see here. You can put a knife in a man and draw it out. It won't matter how many times you say I'm sorry; the wound is still there. A verbal wound is as bad as a physical one."

Friends are very rare jewels, indeed. They brighten our darkest days and encourage us towards success. They lend an ear, they share words of praise, and they always want to open their hearts to us. It is always the right time to show our friends how much we care for them.

Author unknown. (n.d.). Nails in the Fence. Retrieved from https://www.gocivilairpatrol.com/media/cms/Nails_in_the_Fence.

Suggested Reflection and Exercise

1. Personal Reflection:

Think about a time when you lost your temper or said something hurtful to someone close. How did it affect your relationship? Can you recall any attempts you made to make amends, and how successful they were?

2. Broader Perspective:

This story illustrates how anger and harsh words can leave lasting damage, much like nails in a fence. Even when apologies are made, the emotional scars may remain. It reminds us to be mindful of how we express anger and to value and protect our relationships.

3. Questions for Discussion or Writing:

- Why do you think words spoken in anger can cause deep wounds?

- How can we learn to control our temper before it harms others?

- What are some ways to heal or repair relationships damaged by angry words?

4. Suggested Practical Activity:

Keep a small notebook for a week. Each time you feel anger rising, pause and write down what triggered it and how you responded. At the end of the week, reflect on patterns and think of strategies to better manage your reactions in the future.

Stress Management

A lecturer was attempting to explain stress management to his audience.

He raised a glass of water and asked, "How heavy is this glass of water?"

Many called out answers ranging from 20g to 500g.

The lecturer replied, "The absolute weight doesn't matter. It depends on how long you try to hold it. If I hold it for a minute, that's not a problem. If I hold it for an hour, I'll have an ache in my right arm. If I hold it for a day, you'll have to call an ambulance. In each case, it's the same weight, but the longer I hold it, the heavier it becomes."

He paused for a moment, and then continued, "And that's the way it is with stress management. If we carry our burdens all the time, sooner or later, as the burden becomes increasingly heavy, we won't be able to carry on. As with the glass of water, you have to put it down for a while and rest before holding it again. When we're refreshed, we can carry on with the burden. So, before you return home tonight, put the burden of work down. Don't carry it home. You can pick it up tomorrow. Whatever burdens you're carrying now, let them down for a moment if you can. Relax and pick them up later after you've rested. Life is short: enjoy it!"

He went on to share some ways of dealing with the burdens of life:

"You must accept that some days you're the pigeon, and some days you're the statue. Always keep your words soft and sweet, just in case you have to eat them. And drive carefully! It's not only cars that can be recalled by their maker. If you can't be kind, at least have the decency to be vague. If you lend someone $20 and never see that person again, it was probably worth it. It may be that your sole purpose in life is simply to serve as a warning to others. Never buy a car you can't push. Never put both feet in your mouth at the same time, because then you won't have a leg to stand on. Nobody cares if you can't dance well. Just get up and dance. When everything's coming your way, you're in the wrong lane. Birthdays are good for you. The more you have, the longer you live. You may be only one person in the world, but you may also be the world to one person. Some mistakes are too much fun to only make once. We could learn a lot from crayons. Some are sharp, some are pretty, some are dull, some have weird names, and all are different colors, but they have to live in the one box all the same. A truly happy person is one who can enjoy the scenery on a detour. Have an awesome day and know that someone has thought about you today; I did!"

BelievePerform. (2013, June 19). Retrieved from https://members.believeperform.com.

Suggested Reflection and Exercise

1. Personal Reflection:

Think about a recent situation where you felt overwhelmed or stressed. How long did you carry that burden before you allowed yourself to rest or seek relief? How did that affect your well-being and productivity?

2. Broader Perspective:

This story highlights how stress, like holding a glass of water, becomes heavier the longer it's carried without relief. Managing stress requires conscious effort to "put down" burdens periodically, rest, and return refreshed. It also reminds us to embrace kindness, humor, and perspective in daily life.

3. Questions for Discussion or Writing:

- What are some effective ways you personally use to "put down" stress temporarily?

- How does changing your perspective on stressful situations help in managing them?

- Why do you think humor and kindness are important tools for stress management?

4. Suggested Practical Activity:

Set a daily reminder to take a 5-minute break where you consciously "put down" any stress or worries—try deep breathing, stretching, or simply sitting quietly. Notice how this affects your mood and focus throughout the day.

The Daffodils

Several times my daughter had telephoned to enthusiastically tell me, "Mother, you must come to see the daffodils before they are over!"

I wanted to go, but it was a two-hour drive from Laguna to Lake Arrowhead.

"I will come next Tuesday," I promised, a little reluctantly, on her third call.

Next Tuesday dawned cold and rainy. Still, I had promised, and reluctantly I drove there. When I finally walked into Carolyn's house, I was welcomed by the joyful sounds of happy children. I delightedly hugged and greeted my grandchildren.

"Forget the daffodils, Carolyn! The road is invisible in these clouds and fog, and there is nothing in the world except you and these children that I want to see badly enough to drive another inch!"

My daughter smiled calmly and said, "We drive in this all the time, Mother."

"Well, you won't get me back on the road until it clears, and then I'm heading for home!" I assured her.

"But first we're going to see the daffodils. It's just a few blocks," assured Carolyn.

"I'll drive. I'm used to this."

So, we set out on the road, although we could scarcely see six feet in front of us.

"Carolyn," I said sternly, "Please turn around."

"It's all right, Mother, I promise. You will never forgive yourself if you miss this experience."

After about twenty minutes, we turned onto a small gravel road and I saw a small church. On the far side of the church, I saw a hand-lettered sign with an arrow that read, "Daffodil Garden". We got out of the car, each took a child's hand, and I followed Carolyn down the path. Then, as we turned a corner, I looked up and gasped. Before me lay the most glorious sight.

It looked as though someone had taken a great vat of gold and poured it over the mountain peak and all its surrounding slopes. The flowers bloomed in majestic, swirling patterns, great ribbons and swaths of deep orange, creamy white, lemon yellow, salmon pink, and saffron and butter yellow. Each different colored variety was planted in large groups so that it swirled and flowed like a river with its own unique hue. There must have been five acres of flowers at least.

"Who did this?" I asked Carolyn.

"Just one woman." Carolyn answered.

"She lives on the property. That's her home." Carolyn pointed to a well-kept cottage, small and modestly sitting in the midst of all that glory. We walked up to the house.

On the patio, we saw a poster. "Answers to the Questions I Know You Are Asking", was the headline. The first answer was a simple one. "50,000 bulbs," it read. The second answer was, "One at a time, by one woman. Two hands, two feet, and one brain." The third was, "Starting in 1958."

For me, that moment was a life-changing experience. I thought of this woman whom I had never met, who, more than forty before, had begun, one bulb at a time, to bring her vision of beauty and joy to an obscure mountaintop. Planting one bulb at a time, year after year, this unknown woman had forever changed the world in which she lived. One day at a time, she had created something of extraordinary magnificence, beauty, and inspiration. The principle her daffodil garden taught is one of the greatest principles of celebration. That is, learning to move toward our goals and desires one step at a time—often just a single baby-step at a time—and learning to love the doing, learning to use the accumulation of time. When we multiply tiny pieces of time with small increments of daily effort, we too will find we can accomplish magnificent things. We can change our world.

"It makes me sad in a way," I admitted to Carolyn.

"What might I have accomplished if I had thought of a wonderful goal thirty-five or forty years ago and had worked away at it 'one bulb at a time' through all those years? Just think what I might have been able to achieve!"

My daughter summed up the message of the day in her usual direct way.

"Start tomorrow," she simply said.

She was right. It's so pointless to think of the lost hours of yesterdays. The way to make learning a lesson of celebration instead of a cause for regret is to only ask, "How can I put this to use today?"

We should all use this Daffodil Principle. Stop waiting...

Until your car or home is paid off.

Until you get a new car or home.

Until your kids leave the house.

Until you go back to school.

Until you finish school.

Until you clean the house.

Until you organize the garage.

Until you clean off your desk.

Until you lose 10 lbs.

Until you gain 10 lbs.

Until you get married.

Until you get a divorce.

Until you have kids.

Until the kids go to school.

Until you retire.

Until summer.

Until spring.

Until winter.

Until fall.

Until you die...

Author unknown. (n.d.). The Daffodils. Retrieved from https://www.sermoncentral.com

Suggested Reflection and Exercise

1. Personal Reflection:

Think about a goal or dream you've been delaying. How does the story of the woman planting 50,000 daffodil bulbs—one at a time—challenge you to start taking small steps toward that goal today? Reflect on your feelings about patience, persistence, and the passage of time.

2. Broader Perspective:

Consider how the idea of "one small step at a time" applies beyond personal goals. How might this principle influence communities, workplaces, or society when it comes to creating lasting change? Reflect on the power of consistent, incremental effort in any area of life.

3. Questions for Discussion or Writing:
- What "bulbs" are you waiting to plant in your life, and what is holding you back?

- How do you typically respond to setbacks or slow progress?

- Can you identify a time when small, steady actions led to a significant achievement?

- How can embracing the "now" help you find joy in your journey?

References

- Aesop. (2006). *Aesop's fables* (L. Gibbs, Trans.). Oxford University Press. (Original work published ca. 6th century BCE)
- Awfi, M (1363, Farsi). *Compendium of Stories* (Jāmeʿ al-Ḥikāyāt). Elmi- Farhangi, Pubishing Compani. Tehran.
- Azar Yazdi, M. (1968). *The Stories of Sheikh Atta*. (Series: Good Stories for Good Children). Amir Kabir. Tehran
- Bateson, M.C. (1990). *Composing a life.* New York: Penguin Books.
- Bergner, R. (1979). The use of systems-oriented illustrative stories in marital psychotherapy. *Family Therapy. 6*, 109-118.
- Bergner R (1999). Status enhancement: A further path to therapeutic change. *American Journal of Psychotherapy, 53*, 201-214.
- Berman, M. & Brown, D. (2000), *The Power of Metaphor*, UK: Crown House Publishing.
- Boyd, B (1991). *Vladimir Nabokov: The American Years.* Princeton University Press.
- Burns. G. W. (2000). *101 Healing Stories: Using Metaphor in Therapy. Trei.* NY.
- Campbell, Joseph (1949). *The Hero with a Thousand Faces*. New York: Bollingen Foundation.
- Coelho, P. (1998). *The Alchemist*. Thorson. London
- Coelho, P. (2007). *Like The Flowing River: Thoughts and Reflections.* Harper Collins Australia
- Coleman, B. (2004). *The Essential Rumi.* Harper San Francisco, 2004) page 253
- Corrigan, P. (2004). How stigma interferes with mental health care. *American Psychologist*, 59, 614-625.
- Covey, S. (2025). *The 7 Habits of Highly Effective People*. Simon & Schuster. Australia
- Cure of the Ego, The: Nimatullahi Sufi Order. (n.d.). https://www.nimatullahi.org/sufi-stories/the-cure-of-the-ego
- De Vos, G. (2003). *Storytelling for young adults*. Libraries Unlimited.
- Ellis, A. (2004). *Rational emotive behavior therapy: It works for me – It can work for you.* Prometheus Books.
- Epictetus. (2008). *Discourses and selected writings* (R. Dobbin, Trans.). Penguin Classics. (Original work published ca. 108 CE)
- Hamilton, M. and Weiss M. (2005). *Children Tell Stories, Teaching and Using Storytelling in the Classroom.* in: Richard C. & Owen, 2005.
- Kopp, R. (1995). *Metaphor therapy: using client generated metaphors in psychotherapy.* Bristol, PA: Brunner – Mazel

- Lessing, Gotthold Ephraim, (1986). *Nathan the Wise.* Translated by Lewis E. Griggs. Indianapolis: Hackett Publishing Company.
- Mehdevi, A. S. (1980). *Persian folk and fairy tales* (P. E. Kennedy, Illus.). Pantheon Books.
- Otto. M. (2000). Stories and Metaphors in Cognitive-Behavior Therapy. *Cognitive Behavioral Practice 7,* 166-172.
- Owen, N. (2000). *Telling Stories for a change.* Standpoints. Paris: Speakeasy Publications.
- Owen, N. (2001). *The magic of metaphor.* Crown House. Publishing limited. UK.
- Pernicano, P. (2015). *Metaphorical Stories for Child Therapy: Of Magic and Miracles.* Jason Aronson, Inc.
- Peseschkian. N (1987). *Positive Psychotherapy: Theory and Practice of a New Method.* Springer Nature B.V.
- Peseschkian. N (2016). *Oriental Stories as Techniques in Positive Psychotherapy.* AuthorHouse. UK.
- Rennie, D. (1994). Storytelling in psychotherapy: The patient's subjective experience. *Psychotherapy, 31,* 234-243.
- Reps, P., & Senzaki, N. (1957). *Zen flesh, Zen bones: A collection of Zen and pre-Zen writings.* Charles E. Tuttle Company.
- Rumi, J. (2004). *The Masnavi, Book One* (J. Mojaddedi, Trans.). Oxford University Press. (Original work published ca. 1258)
- Rumi, J. (2007). *The Masnavi, Book Two* (J. Mojaddedi, Trans.). Oxford University Press.
- Rumi, J. (1926–1940). *The Mathnawí of Jalálu'ddín Rúmí* (R. A. Nicholson, Trans., Vols. 1–8). E.J.W. Gibb Memorial Series.
- Salahi, O. (1379). *The Book of Molla Nasreddin's Humor and Wit.* Nokhostin Publishing Co. Tehran
- Shah, Idries. (1968). *The way of Sufi.* The Octagon Press. London
- Shah, Idries. (1971). *Thinkers of the East.* The Octagon Press. London
- Shah, Idries. (1982). *Tales of Dervishes.* The Octagon Press. London
- Townsend, G. F. (Trans.). (1867). *Aesop's fables.* London, United Kingdom: George Routledge & Sons.
- Wilkinson, J. (n.d.). *The consultant and the shepherd.*
- Wilk4.com. Retrieved July 23, 2025, from https://www.wilk4.com/humor/humorm182.htm

About Dr. Ali Sahebi:

Dr. Ali Sahebi is a clinical psychologist who received his academic training in clinical psychology from the University of Tehran and the University of New South Wales in Sydney.

He served for many years as a professor of clinical psychology at Ferdowsi University of Mashhad and received cognitive therapy training under the supervision of Dr. Albert Ellis. He has also completed formal training in Schema Therapy and Acceptance and Commitment Therapy (ACT) in Australia and the UK.

Over time, Dr. Sahebi joined the Positive Psychology movement and became a committed practitioner and trainer of Choice Theory and Reality Therapy. He founded the Iranian branch of the William Glasser Institute and has translated Dr. Glasser's complete works into Persian.

To date, he has authored and translated 53 books. Among them are five books in the field of metaphor and story-based therapy, including:

1. Metaphor Therapy: Using Metaphors in Psychotherapy
2. The Educational and Therapeutic Use of Stories
3. Life Is All About Storytelling
4. Stories for Thinking
5. By the Shore of the Masnavi

Currently, he co-directs the Better Choice Institute with Dr. Mehdi Eskandari, offering specialized and public psychology programs both in-person and Online.

This book can be the perfect gift for everyone:
Scan this QR code to get your copy of the book.

If you'd like to share your thoughts or feedback with the author, please connect via:

 asahebi@gmail.com

 https://www.betterchoice.ir/

www.ingramcontent.com/pod-product-compliance
Lightning Source LLC
Chambersburg PA
CBHW052205090526
44583CB00017BA/2139